100

ways to
understand your

CAT

100
ways to
understand your
CAT

Roger Tabor

writer and presenter of the BBC's
Cats and *Understanding Cats*

D&C
David and Charles

A DAVID & CHARLES BOOK

David & Charles is a subsidiary of F+W (UK) Ltd., an F+W Publications Inc. company

First published in the UK in 2005

Distributed in North America by F+W Publications, Inc.
4700 East Galbraith Road
Cincinnati, OH 45236
1-800-289-0963

Printed in China by SNP Leefung for David & Charles
Brunel House Newton Abbot Devon

Commissioning Editor Jane Trollope
Editor Jennifer Proverbs
Art Editor Prudence Rogers
Designer Louise Prentice
Production Controller Ros Napper
Project Editor Jo Weeks

Visit our website at
www.davidandcharles.co.uk

David & Charles books are available from all good bookshops; alternatively you can contact our Orderline on (0)1626 334555 or write to us at FREEPOST EX2 110, David & Charles Direct, Newton Abbot, TQ12 4ZZ (no stamp required UK mainland).

Contents

How to use this book

We love cats because of their self-contained characters and independent lifestyles, but these also mean that we tend not to know much about what makes them tick. Whether you have a specific concern about your cat, or would simply like to know more about it, this book will provide you with a better understanding of your feline friend. Within six major subject areas, 100 key aspects of your cat's life are explained, with straightforward cross-referencing to related subjects. Fascinating in-depth features also give insight into the mysterious world of the cat.

HOW CATS WORK

Cat construction

The structure of the cat is directly related to its behaviour as a solitary, semi-arboreal hunter with a partially nocturnal lifestyle. Each part of a cat's body shows adaptations which together make it the hunter supreme, allowing it to stalk, kill and eat its prey with maximum efficiency. In addition, the cat is fiercely territorial, and its body has special mechanisms for leaving and interpreting scent messages around its home range.

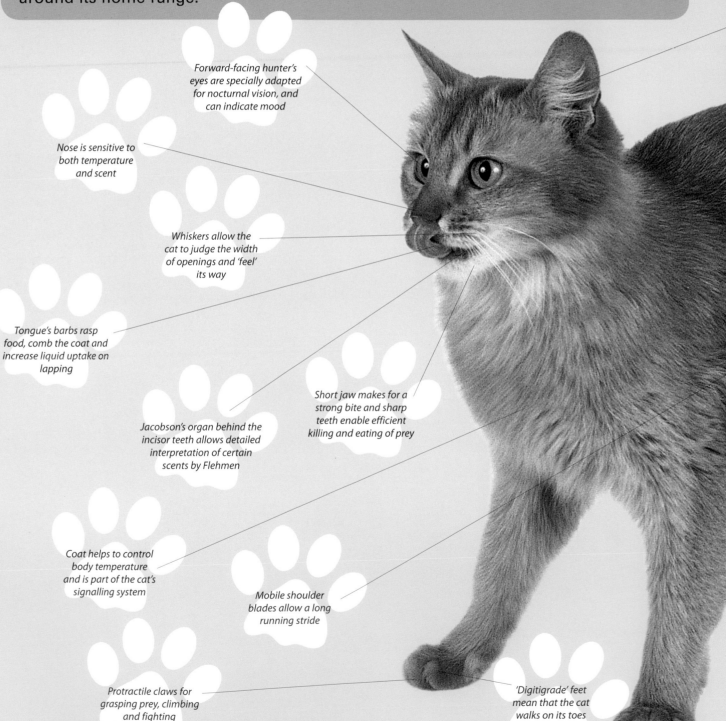

Forward-facing hunter's eyes are specially adapted for nocturnal vision, and can indicate mood

Nose is sensitive to both temperature and scent

Whiskers allow the cat to judge the width of openings and 'feel' its way

Tongue's barbs rasp food, comb the coat and increase liquid uptake on lapping

Jacobson's organ behind the incisor teeth allows detailed interpretation of certain scents by Flehmen

Short jaw makes for a strong bite and sharp teeth enable efficient killing and eating of prey

Coat helps to control body temperature and is part of the cat's signalling system

Mobile shoulder blades allow a long running stride

Protractile claws for grasping prey, climbing and fighting

'Digitigrade' feet mean that the cat walks on its toes – ideal for explosive sprinting

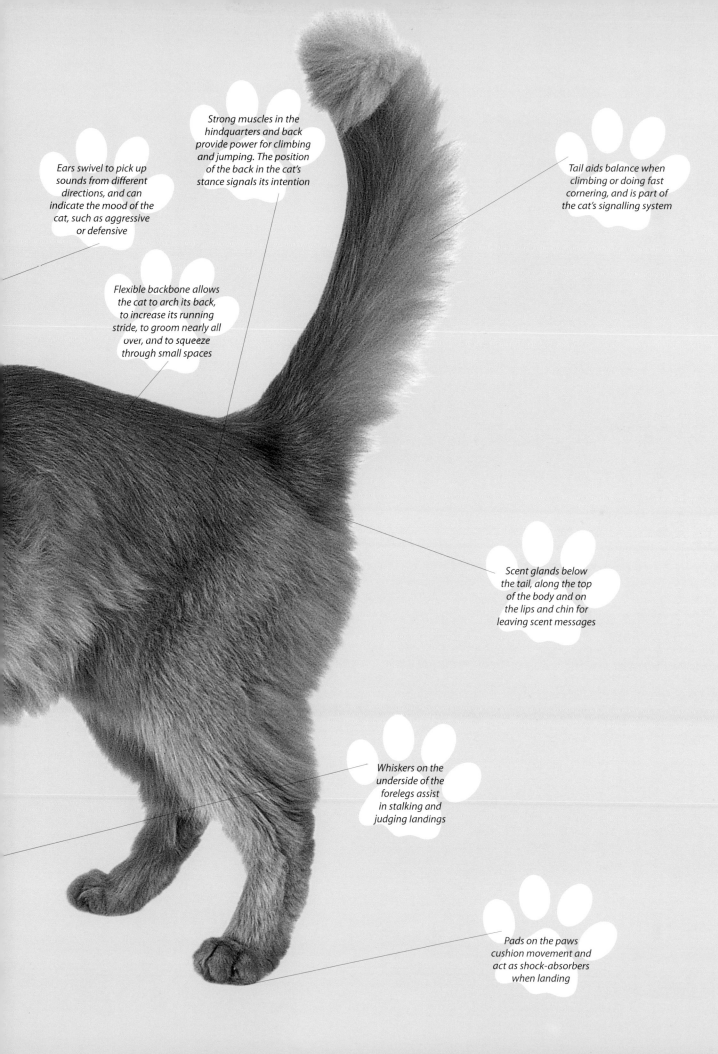

Ears swivel to pick up sounds from different directions, and can indicate the mood of the cat, such as aggressive or defensive

Strong muscles in the hindquarters and back provide power for climbing and jumping. The position of the back in the cat's stance signals its intention

Tail aids balance when climbing or doing fast cornering, and is part of the cat's signalling system

Flexible backbone allows the cat to arch its back, to increase its running stride, to groom nearly all over, and to squeeze through small spaces

Scent glands below the tail, along the top of the body and on the lips and chin for leaving scent messages

Whiskers on the underside of the forelegs assist in stalking and judging landings

Pads on the paws cushion movement and act as shock-absorbers when landing

9

1 Getting about

Fashion's 'cat-walk' is aptly named. On it models lithely parade with the same elegance of movement of a cat. Among the cat's most recognizable feline characteristics is its graceful and sinuous movement. This gives the lone hunter the survival advantage it needs in the pursuit of prey.

Running

The cat is an explosive sprinter – it does not go in for long chases. As a lone hunter it must have the advantage of a variety of movements when in pursuit of its prey. Its shoulder blades are aligned with the side of its body, and it has only a vestigial collarbone, so its shoulders are able to move quite freely, which increases the length of the running stride. During walking, as the forelimbs are placed down on the ground this has a naturally retarding action on the pace, but when running fast, nearly all that effect is lost – the cat extends its forelimbs and arcs down and back before contact is made with the ground. The flexible arching of the cat's spine allows it to extend its stride further by several centimetres.

When a cat is running and galloping the legs are used together in turn on each side of the body. When in full gallop the cat is airborne for most of the extended stride, without any paw touching the ground. When landing between airborne bounds, its forepaws are overtaken by its hindpaws.

Walking

Unlike us who walk on feet with ankles, cats and dogs are digitigrade animals, that is they walk on their toes. This has the effect of both increasing the length of their limbs and reducing the area of contact they have with the ground – a necessary feature for a sprinter. In hoofed animals ground contact is reduced still further to increase their speed, but the cat, being a lone hunter, must retain the ability to manipulate its paws.

During walking, 60 percent of the cat's weight is carried by the forelimbs, and consequently they provide proportionately more support, while the hindlimbs primarily provide propulsion. Cats move alternate opposite paws while walking and tend to have an unhurried air.

related areas...   **2**   **10**   **20**   **21**

2 Jumping

Cats are renowned for their wonderful jumping ability and can leap several times their own length either vertically or horizontally. Their amazing accuracy when landing on a narrow ledge or the top of a fence after a jump is in part thanks to the time that they take to assess it beforehand.

HOW CATS WORK

How a cat jumps

When a cat jumps, whether onto a table, branch or prey, it first takes all its weight onto its hindlimbs, and it is the extension of these that propels its leap. The back and hindquarter muscles are extremely strong and they give the cat its tremendous power to jump up, down, and over a gap or obstacle.

Although a cat has great jumping skills, it needs a firm surface from which to make its leap. It will take some time to size up the jump and will also carefully test the firmness of the take-off with its hind feet, before making a perfectly judged leap. This patient assessment is crucial when the landing place is small or narrow, for example a shelf, windowsill or tree branch, or the gap to be cleared is wide. It is also important when the cat pounces on its prey: here, the judgement is of where the moving prey will be when the cat lands.

related areas...   1   3   22   42

3 Balancing act

The cat's tail is incredibly versatile. It is of particular value in the balance of tree-climbing cats, but also acts as a gyroscopic counterweight when cats corner suddenly after prey, which can be seen most readily in the cheetah, the fastest cat. The tail is also a signalling system and can be fluffed, twitched or wagged to indicate fear, indecision or aggression.

HOW CATS WORK

How cats fall on their feet

The cat's design and build is that of a woodland hunter. Cats move effortlessly among tree branches, aided by the balancing movements of their tail. If their balance is threatened, the tail comes into play. Should they fall, cats have a remarkable ability to land on their feet, which they do by rotating their bodies in mid-air. This is a reflex action and it appears in the kitten in the third week of life, as the youngster's mobility increases.

What happens is this – as the cat falls through the air, it first rotates its head and the front half of its body, until its head has achieved the correct orientation. It then rotates the back end of its body, allowing it to land safely on its feet. The cat is able to carry out this manoeuvre due to its finely attuned sense of balance, which comes from its eye sight (see opposite) and canals in the inner ear (p.15).

It is this same fine sense of 'uprightness' and movement that feeds the cat information on its posture during the dramatic changes of position which take place in the course of a hunt or a fight.

 related areas... 45 46 47

4 Cat's eyes

The eyes are one of the keys to understanding the relationship between cat behaviour and structure. As befits a hunter, the eyes face forward and so, like us, the cat has good three- dimensional and distance evaluation. The all-round vision of herbivorous species allows predators to be seen but lacks the advantages of binocular vision.

Colour vision

In the retina, the cat's visual adaptation to its nocturnal lifestyle has led to a sacrifice of colour discrimination in favour of maximizing light reception. Like us, cats have rod and cone receptors – rods give us vision in low light levels and cones discriminate colour. Three different types of cones work at different wavelengths to interpret the colour spectrum and while we have a ratio of four rods to one cone, cats have 25 rods to each cone. They do retain some degree of colour vision – mostly green with some blue – but after dusk when the landscape is drained of colour (even for us with our better colour vision) the hunting cat has good night vision due to its higher number of rods.

Reducing daylight dazzle

This maximizing of light gathering makes the cat's eye potentially vulnerable to intense light during the day, which is why the pupil closes to a slit instead of a point. This gives the cat much finer control over the gradual closing of the iris. Lions, which hunt mostly during the day, have less nocturnal adaptation and consequently their pupils close to a point, like ours. The degree of dilation of the pupil in a cat is also indicative of mood.

Night sight

The reflective ability of their eyes has given cats a magical air, yet this is just part of the package of night-hunter specialization. The shining-mirror effect is due to a crystal mirror, the *tapetum lucidum*, located behind the retina. In very low light conditions, photons of light stand a greater chance of hitting a light receptor by being reflected back from the tapetum after passing through the retina.

As with other nocturnal hunters, the cat's eye is huge in relation to its skull size, and compared to that of daytime animals, including us. The lens itself and the cornea in front of it are large relative to the back of the eye. The lens is also set back from the front of the eye, which you can see by looking at a cat's eye in profile; the position of the lens can make the eyes seem quite 'glassy' compared to ours. This position gives the eye of the cat a wide aperture and so a greater light-gathering ability. At low light intensity the pupil becomes huge to allow in more light. The cat can see with a sixth of the amount of light that we need.

Daytime living animals have circular pupils controlled by circular fibres that cannot close fully to zero aperture. However, the slit pupils of the nocturnally adapted cat are pulled together by crossing fibres and can close completely

5 The cat's whiskers

Whiskers are very enlarged hairs that are particularly sensitive detectors of touch and air movement. The cat's skin detects contact, and sensory receptors also enable it to feel when guard hairs in the coat brush against an object. The whiskers on the muzzle also move to declare mood and intention, and other cats have no difficulty reading the signs.

Skin and coat

Sensory detectors on the skin vary from as many as 25 to a square centimetre on parts of the head and feet, down to only seven or so per square centimetre on the back, tail and ears. The cat's nose, tongue and paw pads are most sensitive.

The coat can consist of up to 200 hairs per square millimetre of which 150 will be down hairs, 47 awn hairs and 3 guard hairs. The guard hairs and awn hairs protect the cat against the elements. While guard hairs grow singly, both the awn and down hairs grow in clusters that emerge from single hair pores. All these hairs, particularly the guard hairs, are connected to touch detectors, so it is small wonder that a cat combs its hair back into place with its tongue after you stroke it. When a cat moults to produce changes of coat density to match the season, the new hair grows in the same follicle shaft and forces out the old hair.

Whiskers

The base of the cat's whiskers go three times deeper into the skin for firm attachment than do the longest cat hairs. They are bedded into individual fibrous capsules attached to their own large arrector muscles. Working together, these muscles allow the cat to sweep its whiskers forward to investigate prey or another cat, or pull them back out of the way. The base of the whisker has four types of nerve receptors so when the whisker is deflected the cat can accurately feel the degree of pressure, its direction, speed and duration. In particular, the muzzle whiskers are brought into play when a cat is in close contact with small prey. They enable the cat to interpret movement and shape of the prey, and even the direction of the lay of its coat.

As part of its adaptation to nocturnal hunting, the cat's whiskers are sensitive enough to pick up air movements and allow the cat to move through small gaps, such as in woodland conditions or in fencing. The cat also has a tuft of whiskers on the underside of the forelegs. Usually overlooked, these assist in stalking prey and in gauging landing from a leap.

related areas...   7   11   27   28   43

6

Hearing a pin drop

For a night-hunting animal, finely attuned hearing is vital. When a cat hears prey, it is instantly alert, with pricked up ears. There are over 20 muscles that work the pinna, or cone – the exterior part of the ear. The cat uses these muscles to move its ears into a variety of positions to convey its moods and intentions.

Sound detection

Cats are always aware of sound. When your cat is standing in front of you, apparently oblivious to what is behind it, look at its ears and you will probably find that they are pricked towards you. However, at a noise elsewhere, the ears will instantly position more definitely in that direction. The muscles can pivot the pinnae like radar dishes, swivelling them into place to pick up the slightest rustle. As cats can pinpoint the sources of sounds much more accurately when stationary than when on the move, they will often freeze in position while they listen carefully. On the outer edge of the pinna is a flattened pocket of skin, the bursa, which allows the ear to fold and move and may also dampen complex sounds received from behind the head.

Sound is funnelled down from the pinnae to the eardrum and vibrates against a group of small bones in the middle ear. These pass on and amplify the vibrations to another drum at the base of the fluid-filled cochlea in the inner ear. Vibrations are detected by hair cells in the cochleal walls. The cat has an observable operating upper limit of 60kHz. This is significantly higher than the operating upper limit of both dogs (15–35kHz) and people (15–20kHz), encompassing the high-pitched sounds of rodent squeaks, which are in the 20–50kHz range. The large bulbs positioned at the back of a cat's head at the base of the skull are the auditory bulla, and it is thought that these selectively resonate to the sounds made by rodents.

Hearing and balance

The cat's acute sense of balance and movement is achieved through its ears, via the vestibular system – the group of three semi-circular canals in the inner ear. These are filled with fluid, which tends to stay in position through inertia, despite the twists and turns of the cat. Projecting from the walls of the canals are sensory hairs that detect the surge of relative movement between the cat and the fluid. The canals are set at different angles, so movement in any direction is picked up. When a cat is falling, it needs an awareness of when it is the right way up. This is provided in part by calcium particles in the fluid of the semi-circular canals landing on the hair cells.

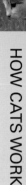

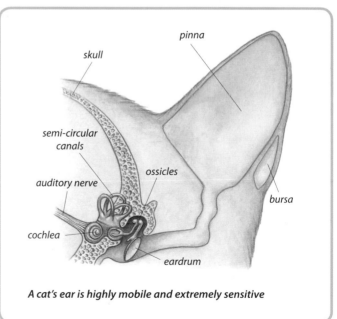

A cat's ear is highly mobile and extremely sensitive

7 Smelling and tasting

The cat's sense of smell is an essential tool in identifying strangers, marking group members (which can include us) and interpreting scent messages left around the home range by other cats. It is also important in determining the cat's response to food before tasting and eating it. A cat can also 'taste' scent using Jacobson's organ (see opposite).

The nose

Inside the cat's nose, separated by a nasal septum, is a labyrinth of bony, plate-like projections, the conchae, which almost fill the space. These are covered by an olfactory mucous membrane creating a surface area of around 20–40cm sq (8–16in sq) – twice the amount found in humans. The olfactory cells in the mucus membrane at the top back of the nasal cavity are capable of detecting volatile substances, but air only penetrates to this area on definite sniffing – rather than simple breathing – by the cat. The cat's ability to detect scent is greater when air temperature is lower than ground temperature, such as occurs in the evening.

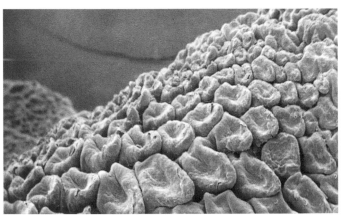

Taste and the tongue

Whenever a cat licks your hand, you are in direct contact with one of the cat's most useful tools – its tongue – and it is a rough contact! In tigers as well as tabbies, the middle of the tongue is covered with backward-pointing spines, or papillae (lower picture), that act as a rasp to break off and assist in gripping meat. The papillae increase the cat's ability to take up liquid through improved surface tension and are also used by the cat for combing its coat.

Taste receptors are positioned on the tip, back and sides of the tongue only. Most mammals can interpret the range of sweet, sour, salty and bitter tastes, but the cat – as a pure meat eater – has hardly any sweet receptors. A cat's digestion can be upset by sweet foods – if it will eat them at all. Kittens do receive milk sugar, lactose, when suckling from their mother, but lactose levels that cause no problems to newborns can cause severe diarrhoea in weaning kittens. Milk is a major cause of diarrhoea in many cats.

related areas... 8 18 19 28

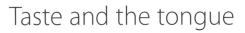

8 An additional sense

Along with many other animals, including horses, cats have an organ – the Jacobson organ – on the floor of the nasal cavity. This organ opens to the mouth, just behind the first incisor teeth on the top jaw and it enables the cat to 'taste' scent. It is mainly used by a male cat to sniff urine and thus interpret the sexual condition of females.

The flehmen response

Named after the Danish doctor who discovered it almost 200 years ago, the Jacobson organ, also called the vomeronasal organ, consists of a pair of blind-ended sacs. To enable air to enter these sacs, the cat adopts a curious, grimacing pose with its mouth partly open – the flehmen response. (Flehmen is a German word that has no ready counterpart in English; 'grimacing', the nearest equivalent, hardly conveys the action.) This has the effect of closing its normal breathing route and instead draws air through the ducts situated behind the incisor teeth, allowing the scented air to be checked. Sometimes the cat flickers its tongue to aid wafting of the scent. The tiger's flehmen response to urine is most dramatic, as it pulls back its lip and exposes its huge teeth. That of the domestic cat is more subtle, so much so that most owners have never noticed it.

We also have a Jacobson's organ, but it is only rudimentary in humans, so we cannot appreciate the information it could yield. However, in most animals it seems strongly linked with sexual behaviour. The organ is connected to the medial hypothalamus, which is involved in sexual activity, and the ventro-medial nucleus, which is involved with feeding control. Because of the territorially dispersed nature of cats, it is likely that the flehmen response is important for males to be able to accurately evaluate a queen's sexual status. Although other males from further afield will eventually gather information on the queen, the resident males will have the advantage, being on the spot to detect early changes in pro-oestrus, ahead of non-group males. When a queen is already in oestrus, the rolling and treading behaviour that toms evoke in her can also be stimulated by the urine spray mark of a tom.

9 Teeth

When a cat yawns, its whole set of teeth can be seen. The most noticeable are the large stabbing teeth. Linnaeus, deviser of the modern system of naming species, referred to the long teeth of the cat as 'canines', but this is misleading for they are more dramatic in the cat family than in the dog family.

HOW CATS WORK

How the jaw works

In comparison with dogs, a cat's jaw is short, and this is because evolution has sacrificed skull length in favour of a more powerful bite (seen below in an African wildcat). Due to its hinging mechanism, the cat's jaw has virtually no lateral movement and this makes its gripping bite doubly effective. One result of the shorter jaw is a flatter face and a related inability in the cat to see what is right in front of its mouth, despite having good vision at a distance. Like the cat, our vision is limited in front of our mouths and like the cat, our adaptation to this is to have flexible front feet (or in the case of humans – hands).

The cat's eating equipment is that of a dedicated hunter. Once prey has been caught and killed, the number and formation of the teeth assist in making possible a shearing action: cats have a reduced number of molars, and the premolars are aligned like serrated scissors to cut through flesh. Cats have no facility to grind food. It is because of this that they adopt a strange, gulping manner when eating grass and leaves.

Sabre-toothed tiger

The first big group of Felidae (members of the cat family) to become established were the sabre-toothed cats. These came into existence around 34 million years ago, when many large mammals developed as the world's climate cooled. At first sight, the sabre-toothed cats seem an unlikely product of evolution, for it would seem that those enormous teeth would have been a great hindrance to eating by blocking the mouth. But, they are one of the cat's great success stories, for the sabre-tooth was the dominant type of cat from the Miocene to the end of the Pliocene. Some sabre-toothed cats were still about only 13,000 years ago, so they survived for nearly 34 million years. In comparison, many modern cats (and mankind) have been around for only a brief time.

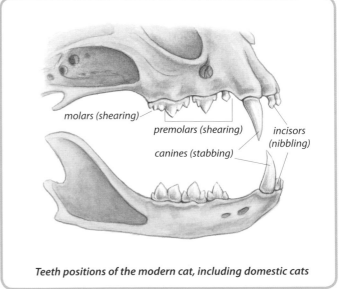

molars (shearing)

premolars (shearing)

incisors (nibbling)

canines (stabbing)

Teeth positions of the modern cat, including domestic cats

10 Paws and claws

Cats rely on their claws for catching and holding their prey when hunting and for grip while climbing. They lavish plenty of attention on these 'tools', frequently washing their paws and sharpening their claws. They also sheath their claws, which protects them from damage and keeps them sharp.

Claws

It is more than just flexibility that enables cats to grip with their front paws: they have protractile claws, like blades, that can simultaneously 'fire' from each paw. (To call them retractile is to misunderstand the animal's behaviour.) In a normal relaxed state, the claw is sheathed, but when the paw is extended ready to strike (in a similar move to our opening our hands wide) the curved claws project. Consequently, while a wolf or dog's first contact with its prey is through its teeth, a cat's is via protracted claws on extended forelimbs. As ever, structure and behaviour are intimately linked.

The claws are also useful crampons for the semi-arboreal cat. The ultimate specialist in tree climbing is the Margay, which lives in the rainforest of South America. Protractile claws allow most cats to climb up trees fairly easily, but they are less able to clamber down with the same grace, as the claws are one-way hooks. The unique Margay is able to walk down a trunk as easily as it climbs up due to the flexible ankles in its hind legs, which allow its back feet to be reversed.

For climbing, as well as for prey-catching and fighting, the effectiveness of the claws is increased if they are sharp, and this is the main reason why cats claw trees. As they drag them through the bark, curved slivers of keratin flake from the sides of the claws, bringing them to a point again.

Paws

Cat's paws consist of four rounded pads, one below each of the toe bones, and a large central pad below the metacarpals and metatarsals. These pads cushion movement and are the prime shock-absorbers when a cat lands from a jump. For further protection, the skin of the pads has an outer layer – the epidermis – that is some 70 times thicker than skin elsewhere on the body.

The pads of the paws are kept soft and supple by watery eccrine sweat glands. When a cat washes its paws, the curious pad pulling and sucking alarms some owners, but it is perfectly normal. Cat's feet are clearly sensitive as they are very choosy about surfaces that they are happy to walk on, often skirting around sharp gravels and rough mats.

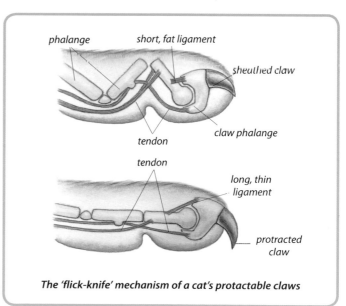

The 'flick-knife' mechanism of a cat's protactable claws

related areas...　9　18　21　22　57　93　96

Do cats have an intellect?

While the seventeenth-century philosopher Descartes is celebrated for his assertion 'I think, therefore I am', he was less flattering towards animals and their behaviour, regarding them as merely automatons. In this, he agreed with the contemporary dogma of mainstream European Christianity, unchanged since the time of St Thomas Aquinas, who propounded the theory that animals were devoid of free will.

Instinct versus free will

To keep themselves 'pure' from anthropomorphic interpretations of animal thought and judgement, many people – including numerous modern-day biologists – have been content to continue to attribute the functioning of animals solely to 'instinct'. The naturalist Charles Darwin was more rational, and suggested that instinct could be thought of as acting in a reflex way. He argued that 'animals possess some power of reasoning', and that 'the difference in mind between man and the higher animals, great as it is, certainly is one of degree and not of kind'. Unfortunately, much of the debate over whether animals act on instinct or intelligence has foundered on the obsessive belief that it must be all one or all the other. In addition, the methodology used in trying to unravel the tangle has been suspect. In 1911, the American psychologist E.L. Thorndike published his book *Animal Intelligence*, in which he described using puzzle boxes to test intelligence. Cats and other species were placed in these boxes and had to push levers or pull string to escape. He described their approach to getting out as a matter of 'trial and error' and the phrase has stuck. His interpretation of his findings was that a cat's approach to the problem was quite 'mechanical', and that any random success was then adopted. His interpretations, and in particular his non-cat friendly experiments, have since been questioned: pushing levers in this manner is quite inappropriate to the cat's way of life. Gradually, laboratory testing has given way to the more realistic practice of observing animals in their natural environment, and from this it seems that, like us, cats use a mixture of both instinct and intelligence.

How a cat learns

Designers of animal IQ tests – and dog owners – maintain that cats score badly compared to dogs. However, this is an unwarranted slur, as such results were simply reflections of the trainability of dogs, measured against the unresponsive nature of cats in the same situation. This, in turn, arises from the biological disposition within dogs to form a group or pack. Such behaviour is not relevant to the cat's more solitary hunting lifestyle,

where it has to make individual evaluations about a situation and then act on them. An individual dog is a cog in a machine, while the cat is the entire machine. In addition, because of their more solitary lifestyles, cats are not as hierarchical in their social organization as dogs, which means they do not have the need to be submissive – in other words they do not need to learn to be obedient.

When the true nature of the cat and how it lives and survives is understood, it becomes clear that it is meaningless to a cat to receive instruction in what to do; cats simply do not have a suitable mechanism for learning like this. Yet when they are self-motivated, they can easily accomplish 'tricks' similar to those of dogs – opening door latches, following elaborate routes, and so on.

Long-lived mammals have lengthy periods of development after birth. Kittens are born at an early stage of development compared to some other mammals, so they have a relatively long rearing period within which their instincts

may be tempered by environmental influences, fitting the adult cat better for its local conditions. Most significantly this tempering of instinctive behaviour has enabled cats to integrate with each other and other animals better than might have been anticipated for relatively solitary carnivores. And this is why we can keep them as pets – the period of littermate socialization (see p.60) has been high-jacked by cat owners.

Territorial behaviour

A good example of how a cat's instincts are altered by environmental conditions is its territorial behaviour. It used to be thought that cats patrolled the boundaries of their territory, but this belief has been superseded by the idea that cats spend more time in areas in which they are confident, due to marking. This suggests that a limited number of inherited (instinctive) imperatives produce the basis of territorial behaviour in cats. The key

ones being: stay in areas in which you feel more confident; travel more if you need more food. Although instincts might provide a framework for such behaviour, a real landscape is made up of features with changing parameters, so the ability to learn about and interpret what it finds gives the cat much more flexibility.

11 Brain

When it comes to brains, relative size – the brain-to-body ratio – is important, and cats have a proportionally larger brain-to-body ratio than, say, rats or mice, so they should have the advantage: larger brains not only have more brain cells, but also many more connections between those cells.

Brain structure

The cat brain consists of three main sections: the forebrain, midbrain and hindbrain. If the brain is viewed from above, the visible surface is dominated by two structures: the cerebellum of the hindbrain, and the cerebral cortex of the forebrain. Like that of most mammals, the cerebellum of the cat is highly convoluted. It is proportionally larger than that of most mammals, however, and specifically controls the co-ordination of movement, balance and posture – vital for a tree-climbing predator.

In large mammals, such as whales and man, the cerebral cortex surface is highly folded, while in smaller animals, like rats or rabbits, there is very little folding. The cat's cortex is significantly folded into a series of ridges, consistent with the cat being quick to investigate and learn, and playful when young.

The surface of the cerebral hemispheres has been mapped into areas that receive information from sense receptors, and areas that control movements of the body. Generally, the larger these areas are in relation to each other, the more brain cells are involved with that function, which in turn reflects its importance to the animal. The nocturnal hunting cat, with its ears finely attuned to the small sounds made by wood mice at night, has a proportionally large area dedicated to receiving and interpreting aural information (25 percent, compared to 10 percent for a rat). The sense of touch originates from the skin, and a map of the cortex area for the relevant sensory neurones reveals a distorted picture of the cat – areas that manage the head and tongue, which require greater sensitivity and have more nerve endings, are correspondingly larger.

Brain development

It is notable that newborn kittens have little folding of the cerebral cortex compared to adult cats. Cat brains grow rapidly through kittenhood, so that by three months when they are gaining an adult size of 20–30g (¾–1oz) the brain is five times larger in volume than when they were born. It is not surprising, therefore, that lack of adequate nutrition during kittenhood can seriously damage cat behaviour patterns.

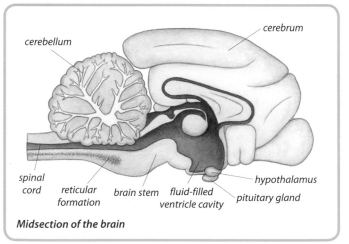

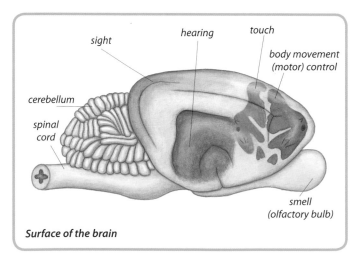

Surface of the brain

Midsection of the brain

related areas...

4 5 6 7

12 Fight and flight

The limbic system resides in the older part of the brain, which consists of the hindbrain, midbrain and lower forebrain. The limbic system is connected with pleasure and avoidance of pain. The hypothalamus and pituitary gland are part of it and are strongly involved with emotional states.

These cause directly opposite effects to each other, so that the aggressive cat's pupils are constricted by the action of the parasympathetic nerves, while the defensive, fearful cat's pupils are dilated by the action of the sympathetic nerves. The relaxed cat's normal pupil size is due to the balancing of the two types of input. Sympathetic nerve endings release noradrenaline (a hormone also produced by the adrenal gland) to the muscles to cause their effect. The adrenal gland affects the body's stress response, producing cortisone, which changes the metabolic rate in territorial disputes and confinement. Adrenaline triggers the fight or flight response, mobilizing the cat's anxiety, fear and aggression.

Other hormones are responsible for different aspects of a cat's daily life. For example, trophic hormones control much of the cat's sexual activity and its timing. During mating, the sensory nerves send a message to the brain and hypothalamus, which triggers the release of luteinizing hormone from the pituitary gland, which in turn causes the final maturing of the ovarian follicles and so the release of the ova.

The hypothalamus

The hypothalamus is the link between hormone control and the brain. It triggers the release of trophic hormones from the pituitary gland, and this causes other glands to release their hormones into the cat's bloodstream, from where they have a general effect on its body. Hormones such as adrenalin, which is produced by the adrenal glands, mediate many of the physiological events that occur during an emotional reaction. Similarly, testosterone, released by the testes, affects the behaviour and build of a tom cat.

The circulating levels of hormones feed back to the hypothalamus and pituitary gland, which adjusts production of the trophic hormones as necessary. Because of its ability to regulate the other glands, the pituitary has been called the 'controller gland'.

Nervous control

The more instantaneous reactions of the body – the flight or fight situations – are controlled by the autonomic nervous system. Involuntary muscles, such as those of the cat's eyes, have a double nerve supply with matching nerve endings in both the parasympathetic and sympathetic nervous system.

HOW CATS WORK

related areas...   18   19   29   31   50   51

13 Acting on instinct

Linked to its effect on hormone release (see p.23), the hypothalamus seems to control the instinctive behaviour that is innate in an animal. Basic functions like eating, drinking and copulation are all triggered here, as well as behaviours involving dramatic emotions of rage, aggression, fear and so on.

HOW CATS WORK

Instinct or learning?

In the past, psychology researchers found that by stimulating the hypothalamus they could cause cats to retract their ears, crouch, growl, raise their backs and lash their tails in a stereotyped reflex manner. With cats that did not normally attack rats, similar stimulation of the hypothalamus would incite the cat to initiate an attack, and kill the rat. However, the attack lacked the skill and refinement of a learned approach, being instead mechanically direct, and had the appearance of an instinctive behaviour pattern.

All this implies that we can distinguish between instinctive and learned behaviour because the sites that appear to control the two are in separate parts of the brain – the instinctive in the older brain and the learned in the newer, developed brain. Equally implicit is that the behaviour produced by dramatic emotion stems from an ancient part of the brain that is remarkably similar in cats and us. Consequently, it is in the grand passions or emotions that our feelings are identifiably most similar to those of the cat.

related areas...

14 15

14 Memory

The dismissive attitude of Descartes and his forebears towards the ability of animals to think, in whatever form, is behind many people's ill-held belief that animals don't have memories (see p.20). However, it can be demonstrated that cats do have a memory and they use it in their relationships with humans.

Pavlov's dogs

Cats, like dogs, show classic Pavlovian conditioning when they suddenly appear at the exact time that you normally feed them. By ringing a bell when he fed them, Pavlov trained his dogs to salivate when a bell was rung. Then, when the bell was rung alone, they still arrived for food and so demonstrated the memory connection. When cats anticipate their feeding time (almost to the minute if you do it regularly enough), they are demonstrating a connection with a time, rather than a bell.

When the clocks are put back or forward with the changing seasons, cats everywhere are confused about their mealtimes. Your cat accurately awaiting your arrival when you regularly return home at a certain time (above) is another example of their ability to remember events.

related areas... 11 39 57 79 25

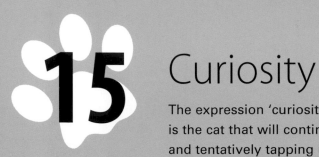
The expression 'curiosity killed the cat' reflects a long-held belief that of all animals it is the cat that will continually show curiosity – exploring, creeping into hidden places and tentatively tapping unusual objects with its paws to test their responsiveness. This behaviour is not without potential risks, as the proverb makes quite clear.

HOW CATS WORK

The link with learning

Young cats are extremely inquisitive. Although it sometimes leads them into difficulties, this appetite for discovery has a very practical purpose. The young cat must learn about the world very quickly: it has about six months, maybe less, in which to prepare itself for life as an adult, and find out how to hunt and deal efficiently with prey, familiarize itself with its environment and keep out of trouble.

Investigation of new objects forms part of some cat play sequences and is particularly noticeable in post-weaned kittens around 10 weeks of age. It is also part of a youngster's development to learn how to check out the state of small prey. This continues into adulthood. For the small-prey hunting cat, continuous curiosity is essential (between naps!) as it must always be on the lookout for potential food. During a hunting sequence and the dazing of prey that follows capture, the cat exhibits both alertness and caution. The slightest small movement alerts a cat, while stillness from the prey invokes a tentative paw tap to test its state of awareness. Sudden movement from the prey brings about the resumption of the chase.

A cat's responsiveness to small movements is exploited by those who like to play 'cat and mouse' games, teasing their cat with a piece of string, or any one of a number of commercially available toys. Other things that intrigue cats and encourage their curiosity to get the better of them include cardboard boxes, which cats love because they are warm and cat-sized, and cars, which smell of us and are associated with plenty of activity on our part. Cats will warily investigate a car's interior. Some cats also appear to watch TV. Their attention is drawn to movements on the screen that correspond to the speed of potential prey, that are 10 times faster than we would notice.

Hunting versus hunger

Paul Leyhausen demonstrated that in the cat the urge to catch goes beyond the immediate need for food. He released one mouse after another in front of a caged cat and found that it was ever ready to catch more. When it had a number in its mouth, and one under each forepaw, it still tried to continue catching. Leyhausen suggested that this is because there is a ranking in drives for survival, and that hunting scores over hunger. For a feline hunter of small prey, the urge to hunt is vital for survival. It produces behaviour that is often termed 'curiosity' by owners, such as the readiness with which a cat will run to the refrigerator (or wherever its food is kept) whenever it opens, showing interest even when it isn't hungry.

related areas...   17   21   22   39   40

16 It's in the genes

Cat genetics are not simple, but they follow a basic pattern – even if it is full of exceptions. In the early twentieth century, biologists stumbled on the obscurely published work of Gregor Mendel who had discovered the principles of heredity in the 1860s. He found that characteristics are inherited by means of units we now call 'genes'.

Coat colour

Genes are linked together in chromosomes, which are made of DNA. Every body cell of the cat has 19 pairs of chromosomes. Sex cells have only 19 chromosomes each; when they divide, parts of one half of the divided chromosome may swap with parts of the other, which randomizes the genetic components. When adult sex cells fuse together on fertilization, they re-form a full complement of 38 chromosomes.

Each kitten inherits a gene for each characteristic from both of its parents. When cats were first domesticated, they were all mackerel tabbies – their coat colour genes were identical. However, very rarely, mutations can occur, and these 'mistakes' in the genes are the origin of the range of coats and colours in domestic cats today.

The earliest coat mutation was black, melanism. The offspring of two apparently identical tabbies might include a black kitten or another solid colour kitten among a litter of mainly tabbies. Usually, one coat colour is dominant over another, which is termed recessive. Tabby is dominant over black, so if a tabby and a black cat mated, their offspring would all be tabby, but if two of these offspring mated together there would be both tabby and black kittens. However, genetically all domestic cats remain tabbies. Even in a solid-coloured cat, you can still see the tabby stripes in certain lights. Some colours occur as a result of additional genes modifying others. For example, black is turned to chocolate by a further recessive gene.

The ginger gene

It is usually assumed that genes are inherited randomly, but some genes are on the same chromosome and are, therefore, inherited together. One pair of the chromosomes dictate a cat's sex – females have a matched pair of chromosomes, XX, while males have an X and a Y. The Y is smaller than the X, while the rest of the chromosomes occur in matched pairs. Every ovum has an X chromosome, but a sperm can have either an X or a Y chromosome. Consequently, any mutation carried on a sex chromosome will be 'sex-linked', and this is what happens with ginger. The Y chromosome does not have a site for an orange gene, so a male can only transmit it on the X chromosome, and can only be orange (O) or non-orange (o). In contrast, a female, with two sites, can be orange (OO), tortoiseshell (Oo) or non-orange (oo).

Incomplete dominance

While most genetics work on the all-or-nothing basis of dominance or recessive, the notable exception is 'incomplete dominance', in which both genes function but neither is dominant. The prime examples are the pointed cats of South East Asia. When a seal-point Siamese is crossed with a traditional Burmese, a midway colour appears – a less full colour form of Burmese, but with colouring to the points – the Tonkinese.

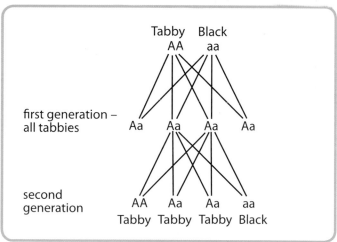

Tabby   Black
AA   aa

first generation – all tabbies   Aa   Aa   Aa   Aa

second generation   AA   Aa   Aa   aa
Tabby   Tabby   Tabby   Black

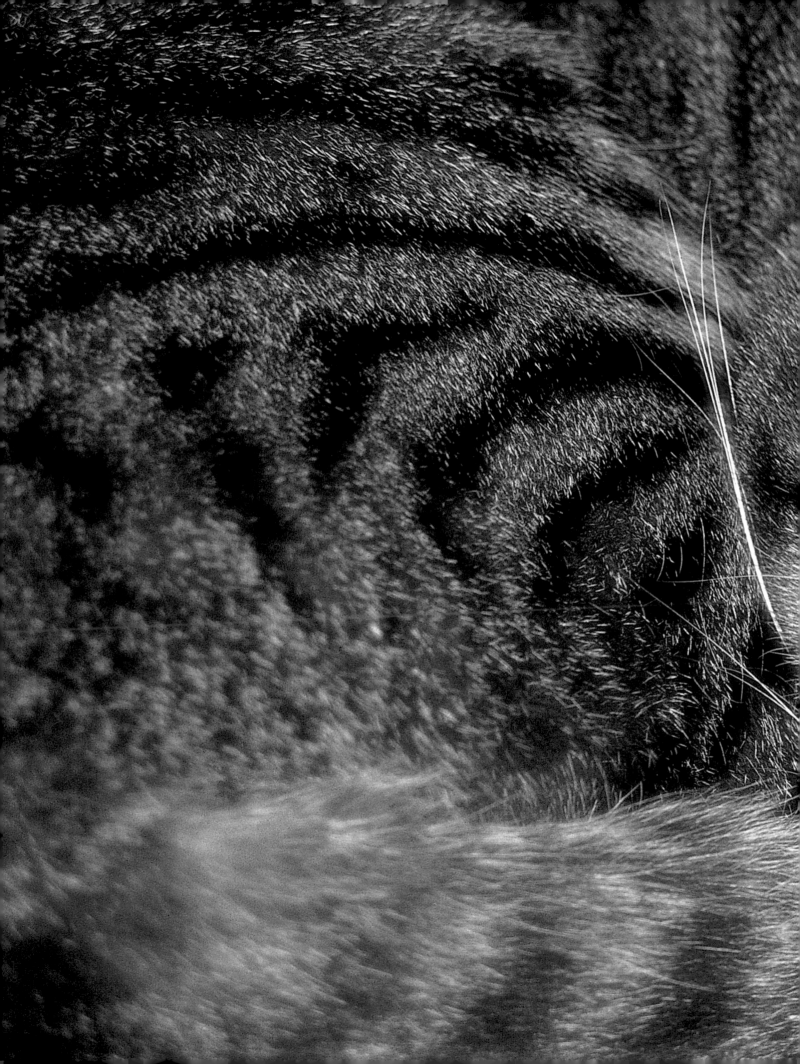

A CAT'S LIFE

The territorial cat

Territory and range are words that are very often used interchangeably by cat owners, yet to a cat biologist they mean very different things: the territory is the area that a cat will defend against other cats, while the range is the area the cat normally inhabits. Territories are usually a bit smaller than the normal home range. The concepts of territory and home range vary according to the type of animal.

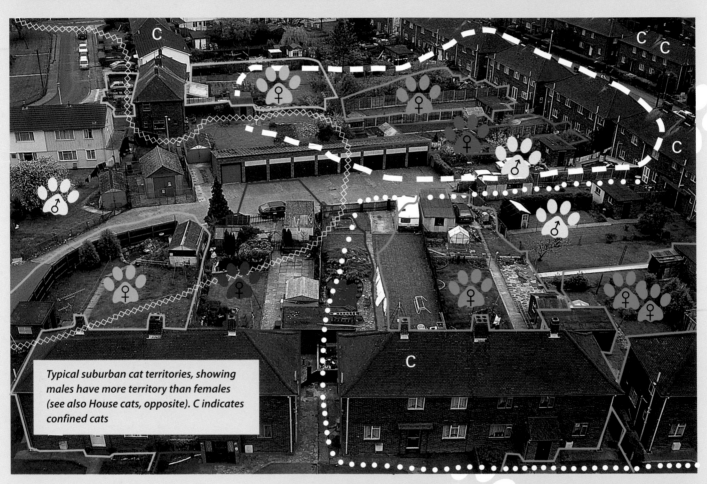

Typical suburban cat territories, showing males have more territory than females (see also House cats, opposite). C indicates confined cats

The search for food

The need to obtain food is common to all animals, and the landscape they inhabit dictates the availability of food, the best way to obtain it, and consequently the animal's social structure. An open landscape encourages group grazing by herbivores, and hence a group predator (such as our dogs' ancestor, the wolf) is most efficient in hunting such a landscape. In enclosed landscapes, the reverse is true. The home range for lone hunting cats pursuing solitary prey is an individual affair, and in consequence so is the territory.

Home range

I started to investigate feral cat behaviour and home ranges in the 1970s. At that time, cats were considered pets or pests: it was thought if they were not household animals then they must be starving. But my studies revealed that feral cats were not that different healthwise to house cats. My main study, started in 1977, was in Fitzroy Square in the heart of London. The cats scavenged from waste sacks and bins around the square, but obtained a large proportion of their diet from kindly feeders. The male cats maintained home ranges of around 2 hectares (5 acres), while those of the females were a little over 0.2 ha (0.5 acre). The density of cats was around 12 per ha (30 per acre).

I also carried out similar studies on the house cats of densely suburban

his group from other groups, and imparts social stability in a genetically related group of cats. The queen is the basic unit of the cat's pattern of land use. In any area she has the amount of land that is needed to support her; the tom defends a larger area within which those queens he is most likely to mate with can rear their young more securely. Where food is mainly in one place – around waste bins, where a feeder puts it or at a rabbit warren – the cats have a common core area of overlap. Where food is sparse, the queens' ranges do not overlap as much. In the feral cat colony at Fitzroy Square, after neutering the range of one of the males shrank to become the same as that of the females. Following neutering, two other males moved away. Males commonly have a greater tendency to mobility.

House cats

In the lives of suburban cats, the pattern of ranges becomes more cramped because cats view us both as a food source and as some sort of cat. Each house cat forms its own group with its owners, and has a common core area with them in the house. In identifying with her owners as her group, a queen behaves territorially towards a neighbouring queen as if she were a member of another feral group. Toms still overlap a number of queens' ranges, and will set the size of their range relative to these queens. Females have only just a bit more territory than their own garden, while males again have 3 to 10 times as much.

of London. Even though house cats are domestic animals, their ranges have not, until recently, been limited (some people now keep cats permanently indoors) and they can pass through or over boundaries with ease. Yet they do not wander randomly: they set their own territorial limits, keeping a watch over the cat next door. In one study area of nineteenth-century terraced housing and small gardens, with a density of 20 cats per ha (50 per acre), I found the average neutered female to inhabit only 0.029 ha (0.07 acre). The average neutered household tom had 0.11 ha (0.27 acre), while intact toms averaged a bit more at 0.18 ha (0.44 acre). It seemed that our household moggies are prepared to accept smaller ranges than feral town cats.

In contrast, a study of farm cats by David Macdonald and Peter Apps found queens to be using a range of about 6 ha (14.75 acre), with the toms' ranges being much larger. The density was about 100 times lower than that of the city feral cats. This was remarkable, for although one group was feral and the other farm cats, in reality they both had additional feeding

and both were free-ranging. Why should cats live at much higher densities in town? The main answer is the availability of food – the size of the home range of the cat is the area it needs to obtain its food. If food is plentiful, it does not need a large range, but if food is scarce it does. Put simply, the town provides richer pickings than the countryside. The cat is a most competent scavenger and the availability of food from tips and rubbish sacks and being fed by dedicated people has allowed cities to absorb high numbers of feral cats.

Toms and queens

Toms have much larger ranges than queens. Although they are bigger, it is not by much, so their food requirements are not much more, yet their ranges have been found to be 3 to 10 times larger. Studies of wild cats, big and small, have demonstrated the same ratio. My own observations have led me to believe that the reason is social. The male ranges overlap those of the queens of what can be viewed as a group. The male buffers the queens of

A cat's territory is not an absolute size: it varies with the season, and even with which cat it is adjacent to. In winter a house cat may not venture outside much at all. In summer, it will have favoured sunning spots in the garden, as well as shady haunts. It will also have preferred latrine areas and patrolling and guarding points.

Core area

The cat's world inside the house, where we are in contact with it most often, is like the core area of overlapping ranges of a feral group (see pp.30–31). Depending on your use of the garden, the overlap with your cat will vary. Usually queens' ranges approximate to your garden and a little more, while toms wander further afield. A transition occurs between the inside and the outside world when you open the door, or provide a catflap. Flaps can become points of social tension. Generally however, their advantages easily outweigh their disadvantages.

Multi-cat adjustments

As multi-cat households have become more common this has affected our cats' territories – for good as well as bad. When we have more than one cat, our homes become even closer to a real cat group. When a new cat moves in there is a period of territorial adjustment, which can cause stress problems, however, this usually settles after a while. In addition, the more friendly you are with your neighbours, and the more you visit one another and go into each other's gardens, then the more tolerant the cats in each household will grow of each other. It is as if the perception of group size has grown. In such situations, events can occur between neighbouring cats that would normally happen only within a group. For example, when prey is brought back into its garden by a hunting cat, then a neighbour's cat, whose presence has been allowed in the hunter's garden, will take an interest, but unless it is particularly aggressive it is unlikely to intervene. However, if the prey escapes, then not only will the cat who has lost the prey go back over sites in the garden where it had the prey and check them out, so too may the 'group adopted' neighbouring cat.

18 Leaving a mark

As most territories are larger than the cat can see all at once, they are dependent on leaving and interpreting scent messages. The cat has a finely attuned ability to discriminate between scents. We can detect some, such as the spray of a tom (p.34), but others are too subtle for us.

A CAT'S LIFE

Chinning

Chinning is when the cat rubs with the large sebaceous scent glands along its lips and chin. You may find your cat crouched down, extending its chin and rubbing it on the ground. It may be attracted to residual scent from another cat's anal scent glands, or to some other significant scent. Usually the cat will chin in a straightforward way. At other times it acts more obsessively, determinedly sniffing and rubbing. Once its chinning episode is finished the cat will show little further interest in the spot.

Rubbing

Although cats have very few sweat glands, they do have sebaceous glands to protect the hair and provide scent. The glands are on the lips and chin, the top of the head and along the top of the tail. When we stroke a cat or it rubs itself against us, we pick up these scents, gaining a group scent identification.

Watch your cat in the garden. You may find its attention is drawn by scent to a plant tub or low wall. It will sniff carefully for perhaps five seconds, and may then rub where it has been sniffing. It may just rub with its cheeks, or it may continue with the side and then the back of its head. It may then sniff the object again, sometimes repeating the rubbing. With a leafless bush or a stick jutting into its pathway, the cat will spend proportionally more time rubbing with the side of its mouth slightly open. It is also likely to brush against it with its body. This behaviour is called 'allorubbing' and it creates a group identity within cats in multi-cat households and between individuals in feral groups, at the same time as encouraging group bonding.

Clawing

When a cat drags its claws through trees and other wooden objects, to sharpen them, this might also be marking or, as suggested by Dennis Turner, it might be a show of dominance. Cats do it more in front of other cats than when they are alone, but this may be mutual territorial assurance as they also do it in front of owners.

Declaring ownership

Like other forms of marking, spraying is a way for a cat to mark its territory. Athough queens can spray, they do so less often than toms. The spray of an intact tom is extremely pungent and unmistakeable. A neutered tom may well spray in the same way as an intact tom, but the spray will lack the all-invasive odour.

How it's done

When patrolling his territory an intact tom will reverse up to an elevated object, stand tall and lift his rump high and, tail erect and quivering will spray a highly pungent stream of liquid. Among farm cats, it has been found that toms will spray more often when there is a queen in oestrus nearby. The most frequent rate of sprays found by Peter Apps in a tom-patrolling farmland was 63 per hour. At this rate it is clearly not to empty his bladder; patrolling spray volumes are usually quite small.

Corbett studied cats on the island of North Uist, and observed that while patrolling the rabbit burrows, they normally sprayed every 5½ minutes.

Confidence

Spraying, and then reading its own scent and not another, seems to give a cat confidence of territorial ownership. The frequency of spraying can increase in an area of territorial dispute. As they are key crossing points, it may be that doors

with catflaps are specifically sprayed in territorial conflict. As your cat goes through the catflap it leaves grease from its coat on it. Consequently, it will sniff the flap carefully from time to time to check if the scent on it is still its own, or if there has been an intruder. A strange scent can make the cat cautious and take longer to go out than at other times.

The role of spraying in territorial confidence is further seen in the location of patrol spraying. This is carried out in the areas of main use, such as hunting areas, while there are fewer sprayed points at the believed edge of the home range: this highlights the difference between territory and home range (see pp.30–31). Cats do not behave as if they are doing guard duty circuits; rather, it is a matter of confidence and usage. That spraying is in large part for territory declaration is evidenced by the fact that toms spend more time investigating spray from other intact toms of unknown origin than from those of their own or an adjacent group.

It is in a cat's nature to hunt. Even a well-fed house cat has the instinct to stalk prey, pounce and kill. Kittens learn to hunt within a few weeks of their birth and much of their play routines revolve around honing their hunting skills and include pouncing, ambushing, chasing and fast sprints.

Stalking or sleeping?

We usually picture the cat's hunting behaviour as the classic sequence of a stalk, followed by capture leading to the kill. But although the stalk is frequently used to catch birds on the ground, it is not appropriate in every situation. For a garden bird, the cat stalks in a dash-and-freeze method. The cat keeps its body slung so low that its shoulder blades stand high like those of a cheetah. The bird has a range of advantages, including a huge field of vision from eyes on the side of its head, and escape by wings.

Most successful hunts involve small mammals as prey, and while a stalking run is often used, skilled hunting cats are always alert to opportunities even when just strolling around or apparently snoozing. For example, carnivorous shrews must eat every two hours, day and night, winter and summer, and become so focused on their foraging that they are oblivious to the fact that they are rustling among fallen leaves. In contrast, herbivorous voles make trails underneath the mat of grass, and so are out of sight. In both cases, when the cat hears a movement, the potential prey may be less than a metre away. As sound is harder to detect when a cat is moving, it will pinpoint the source by sitting still and tilting its ears. Unaware of the danger, the prey may wander out in front of the cat into the open, but this may inhibit the cat, who may not grab the unwary prey but just paw at it tentatively.

How often cats catch and bring home one species rather than another, or whether they catch anything at all, depends on a number of factors. If they did not learn the skills as a kitten, cats do not normally become competent hunters as adults. Their kitten experience can also give them a facility with species they encountered then. Some prey is easier to catch than others. In spring when fledglings are abundant and their parents are at their busiest, they are vulnerable to capture, as are young inexperienced rabbits when first emerging above ground.

Watching and waiting

House cats are often unperturbed if their prey dashes behind vegetation or some object, and will spend some time trying to dislodge it from its position or simply waiting for it to reappear. If the animal has gone into a burrow, the cat may try to extract the prey with its paws extended. If successful, it will again resort to tentative patting. The cat has every justification for being tentative as a vole or shrew will certainly threaten the cat with its teeth.

'Playing' with prey

When engaged with prey, cats may be seen to 'play' with it. Most critics of cats, and indeed many owners, assume that playing with prey is just an unnecessary exercise in prolonged cruelty. However, there is more to it than first meets the eye: it seems that the cat may be reducing its chances of being injured.

Self-defence

Prey animals are capable of self-defence, and cat behaviour takes this into account. Even in large cats, so-called 'inhibited play' seems to stem from a fear of injury by the prey. Moles will turn defensively onto their backs ready to give a formidable bite, and rats, mice, shrews and voles (see p.37 photograph bottom right) will also bite. Infections arising from such bites could be fatal and are best avoided. Leyhausen found that if a rodent squeaked loudly even when it was touched only lightly, the cat was likely to leave it alone. But, if the cat was hungry, that was another matter! In the gap between capture and dispatch, small birds can fly off, so part of the cats' apparent play behaviour is to limit this.

Dazing the captive

One of the functions of playing with prey is to tire it and make it more vulnerable to a neck bite. This is particularly effective with shrews. When first captured and released they run fast, rather than remaining still, but, as carnivores themselves, they are ready to bite the cat's muzzle. On recapturing a shrew, the cat has to act quickly, while being wary of the bite. As the shrew wearies, its running speed and distance is reduced, although it is ready to defend itself to the last.

To kill its prey a cat usually has to release it and apply a neck bite. As lone hunters, cats have short muzzles to enable stronger bites, so although the cat has excellent vision, due to the flatness of its face, the area around its mouth is virtually invisible. The whiskers may move towards the prey, but this does not overcome the problem of the cat not being able to see what it is doing. In consequence, dazing prey through 'playing', is essential. Once the prey is apparently dazed, the cat needs to be sure that it is actually dazed before risking contact. So it will sit and look around and away from the prey with apparent disinterest. If the prey is not dazed but watching for its moment, it will use this time to flee. The cat will then whirl around and the chase will resume, with the whole procedure being repeated until the prey is sufficiently dazed or has escaped (see also 'Observations on a hunting cat', pp.38–9).

related areas... **2** **4** **5** **20** **22**

The deadly dazing pounce

Once a cat has located the prey it has to act quickly or risk losing its advantage. One of its key hunting skills is the dazing pounce. On capture the cat may seem to play with the prey for a while, but this is partly a protective action (see Self-defence, opposite). Death comes via an accurate bite to the nape.

Pouncing

If a vole manages to evade capture or skips back into the grass, the cat will relocate its position with its ears and then use its vole-dazing pounce. To do this, it rises up on its hind legs and brings its weight down through stiffly held front legs onto the prey. (Foxes make a near-identical movement.) This stunning blow can knock the air out of the vole and cause it to give an involuntary squeak. When the grass is tall, preventing a steady approach and possibly allowing the prey to disappear, the cat may make a distant leap. It will ease its body back without moving its feet and then let fly in a high, curving arc. In hunting a bird, the cat takes fewer chances, but still does not always employ the classic stalk method. If a bird is on a low branch, an experienced cat can sprint, leap and grab the bird in one smooth action.

Killing

While some species of small wild cat deliver a nape bite at once, any cat may go in with paws first, particularly if safety reasons require the prey to be dazed. Domestic cats generally dispatch prey after it has been dazed, although on some occasions the capturing bite is delivered in such a direct way as to kill the prey.

From extensive observations Paul Leyhausen believed that cats normally bite into the cervical spinal cord. He took the following as signs of fatal injury: the prey animal's eyes bulging, the rump and limbs convulsing and the tail stretching stiffly.

The cat's canine teeth are particularly well served with mechano-receptors, so when the teeth make contact with bone when moving across muscle, the cat has the potential to adjust its bite through nerve feedback, inserting a tooth between the vertebrae like a wedge and severing the spinal cord. Using X-ray, Alan Hatch and I examined numerous small mammals killed by cats, and found no sign of vertebrae damage.

related areas...   2   16   21   39   40

Observations on a hunting cat

There are distinctions and similarities in a cat's behaviour when catching a bird and catching a small mammal. I had the opportunity to analyse the two types from films of hunt and capture made without human intervention. It is interesting to note the differences, and learn a little bit more about a cat's hunting technique. In both the cases described here the prey finally escapes the cat.

Cat and bird

The cat captures a young robin and takes it into its own garden (territory). Having picked a specific spot, it lies down and releases the robin. It then taps the bird with its right forepaw and the bird takes off, only to be recaptured within a second. Over the next few minutes this sequence repeats itself several times: the cat lets the bird go, moves away, returns and taps it, it flies away and is then recaptured.

A second cat, a house mate of the first, appears. This distraction allows the bird to flutter away for a metre or so, and the second cat follows it and sniffs at it. The bird remains stock still, a 'nerves of steel' behaviour that is quite normal during the recapture hunt, and has the effect of imposing caution upon the cat. The second cat is not a skilled hunter; instead of attempting to kill the bird, it sniffs and then moves away. The first cat walks 3m (10ft) away from the bird, back to the exact spot where it first positioned it. Such apparent indifference is not uncommon. With a static prey like this the cat seems to follow one of two options: it either re-taps to test the prey's degree of dazedness, or it waits to give the prey time to attempt to flee, a movement that seems to trigger the cat to recapture it. For most recaptures the cat springs up and pulls the bird down with its front paws, the adult version of the kitten's 'bird swat' play move.

At this point, the bird, which has been motionless for nearly 5 minutes, looks around cautiously. This seems to be what the first cat is waiting for; it goes to the bird and sniffs it, then sits down, sniffs the air and looks around. Despite the feigned indifference, it is clear that the cat is watching the bird carefully. After about two minutes, looking at the cat and sensing it can escape, the robin takes off, landing 2.5m (8ft) up on an ivy-clad wall, 6m (20ft) away. The cat pursues and comes back down with the bird in its mouth. Escape to recapture has taken only 10 seconds.

The cat repositions the bird in the original spot, and looks away! However, it looks back just as quickly. The initial glance away is to check its own security, and having looked at the bird it sniffs the air and gives a characteristic quick lick, like a fast flehmen response (p.17) without the gaping. For 30 seconds, the cat repeats this looking and licking, then gets up and moves 1m (3ft) behind the bird. It settles down, and continues to look around and sniff. After a few minutes, it moves back, sniffs the bird briefly, (opposite top) then again sits and looks around. It then puts its left forepaw on the bird's tail (opposite below) and lies down sphinx-like, but remains alert. In a repeat of its earlier tactics, it then taps the bird's back, and the robin responds by flying off. The cat grabs it with a paw, pulling it down to the ground less than ½ second after the bird took off. But as the bird bounces on the ground, it changes direction by 90 degrees and this time evades the cat and flies to freedom. Over the 14-minute sequence the bird made at least 8 escape moves before it finally flew off. A significant proportion of birds escape completely during the course of the 'recapture hunt'.

Cat and small mammal

The same cat brings a field vole back to its garden and releases it in a corner made by a brick and stone step. This is a good strategic place to release the vole so that it can be recaptured and confined. It is an area where the cat feels confident, and knows better than does the prey. The play part of the hunt is similar to that with the bird, but the cat lowers its height several times, by rolling over, seemingly to encourage the vole to move. When it does move, the cat blocks its escape with a paw, but carefully, to avoid a bite. This fear of a bite seems well founded when the cat rolls its head near the vole, which tries to bite the cat's ear as it passes. Shortly afterwards the cat brings its nose down towards the vole, which again threatens with an open mouth. The cat pulls its head back smartly.

The vole makes use of gaps in the bricks to evade the cat, which puts its paw, then its head into the gap. When the vole squeaks, the cat rapidly withdraws. There is another entrance to the gap, which the cat also investigates, moving between the two several times. Using a hooking action, it eventually gets the vole out, positions itself between the hole and the vole, and taps the vole again. The vole sets off across the garden, leaving cover behind. After a metre or so it stops; so does the cat. After 20 seconds the cat taps the vole, which spins around with open mouth and tries to bite the paw (see p.37 bottom right; this dramatic still from the analysed film clearly shows the need for caution by the cat, and that the contest is not as one-sided as it first seems). The sequence is repeated.

Remarkably, the vole then runs directly under the cat, which steps back. The vole goes into the cover of the long grass of the lawn. The cat tentatively taps at the vole, then uses vigorous paw movements, concerned that the vole is escaping. The vole squeaks and the cat becomes cautious. He eventually makes a pounce. This elicits a squeak, so the cat reverts to the prodding and then stops. The cat sits looking around for 30 seconds, sniffs the air a number of times and then suddenly, fixing its ears on the spot, leaps up and makes a more vigorous pounce (see p.37 bottom right). The vole squeaks, so the cat taps it once more before looking around and sniffing the air. The vole makes good its escape, as many small prey do.

During the 11-minute sequence, the vole threatened the cat at least six times, retreating to bricks and long grass. The vole's aim was to find cover, to get away and inhibit the cat's direct attack by threatening to bite.

23 Cats on the hunt

Many cat owners worry about their cats bringing home birds as prey, and many non-cat owners believe that cats are decimating our bird population. Cats, like any predator, catch prey, but this does not simplistically mean that they are having a devastating effect on wildlife. Cats and birds can both thrive in your garden.

A CAT'S LIFE

The truth about cats

Prey is not necessary for the survival of domestic cats and their range sizes (see p.32) are independent of its abundance. While this could make them more of a danger to wildlife, this does not occur for a number of reasons. Firstly, not all house cats are competent hunters, and most only catch prey occasionally. Secondly, city cats – domestic and feral – catch only a fraction of the prey caught by rural cats. (Although cats are superb hunters it is their scavenging ability that allows them to survive as feral animals.) Thirdly, cats catch far more small mammals than they catch birds.

Proportionately, town cats will catch more birds than their country cousins – this is because both birds and cats are more common in towns than they are in the country. As well as keeping cats, we feed the birds, we provide them with artificial nesting sites – in the form of nest boxes and buildings – and our gardens provide good habitat with excellent insect populations and lawns with abundant earthworms. So, in reality, both cats and birds are at a superabundance in suburban areas because we provide food and shelter for both. What is often forgotten is that each year garden birds produce vastly more offspring than can possibly survive, and large numbers die whether from predation or other reasons for the population to stay stable.

Cats and bird tables

Despite the facts as outlined above, you might still feel that to have a bird table in a garden that is frequented by cats is providing the latter with a dining table. However, many people, including me, love

to have both cats and birds about, and it is not as crazy as it sounds.

It is easy to make your bird table less user-friendly to cats. First choose one that doesn't help them in their endeavours. Rustic, wooden-legged tables allow the cat to sprint up them, while smooth metal poles do not. It is also possible to have no pole, and to suspend the table on chains. Poles can have a lampshade-like collar that opens downwards, which is effective against cats. Some people like to keep out grey squirrels and pugnacious starlings as well as cats, and so use a roofed table with wire-netting sides or a similar restrictive access system.

A potential problem with an open platform table, which is what I use, is that if it is positioned anywhere near a fence or wall, cats can leap onto it. Placing it in the centre of a vast expanse of lawn with no form of cover for the birds (or the cats), is not a good option. Birds need

other birds about to convince them that all is well and that it is safe enough to feed. Therefore, an isolated table will remain nearly bird free, while one adjacent to bushes on which a queue of birds can form will receive far more visits. I found that having my table separated from the fence and a tree by a japonica (flowering quince, *Chaenomeles japonica*) works very well. The japonica has a most attractive early and long-lasting flowering season, which is an asset to any garden, and a set of wicked spiny thorns, which cats dislike, yet which allow the birds to queue up comfortably while they are waiting to feed at the table.

As a final note, many of the fears about cats on the bird table are irrational because cats do not catch birds on the table. The real risk is that birds feeding on the ground will be stalked by the cat, so it is better to feed them on the table – and try to avoid spillage.

24 Cat naps

The proportion of sleep in 24 hours relates to the lifestyle of a species; for example, the incredibly slow-moving sloth can spend over 80 percent of its time asleep, while the small hunting shrew has to eat every two hours or die, and so hardly sleeps at all. However, although the cat is also a hunter, its larger size means it is not hostage to sleep loss!

Sleep requirements

While large grazers, from horses through to elephants, sleep remarkably little – perhaps only four or five hours in 24 – as they need to work hard to consume huge quantities of grass and leaves, the protein-rich diet of the cat allows it to invest more heavily in sleep. This probably enhances the cat's longevity, which is greater than would be anticipated from its size alone.

Not only does the cat, with its higher protein intake, sleep more than the dog, but as a lone hunter, it does not have the group support of the dog family. Consequently, it needs a device that will allow it to doze, but then be awake in an instant. The cat has a third eyelid, the translucent nictating membrane, and when the merest shadow crosses it, the cat springs into alert action. Usually the cat has its outer eyelids partly closed so that the eyes do not look strange, but when this is not so, owners unused to seeing completely white, pupil-less eyes may become alarmed.

Kitten safety sleep

As the mother of a new litter has to leave the 'nest' in order to catch food, it is vital in the early days that the young do not move from this safe haven. Consequently, kittens are born in a more immature state than many mammals, with the result that while young they sleep for a proportionally greater part of each 24 hours. This is primarily deep sleep, which lasts for about 12 hours in every 24. After their first month of life, kittens change over to the adult pattern.

related areas...   4   25   26   76

25 Sleep behaviour

Although cats sleep for much of the time, a cat's sleep pattern does not necessarily coincide with our own, as you will have noticed if you have been rudely awakened at 5am by an insistent meowing after your cat has returned from a nocturnal foray. In addition, the cat does not take all its sleep at once, but will snatch a number of cat naps as well.

Sleep patterns

For most animals, sleep patterns follow a biological clock, a circadian rhythm tied to the natural 24-hour cycle of the earth's rotation. Generally, predators restrict their waking activities to the times when they are most likely to encounter their prey. In most parts of the world, and especially in the northern temperate lands, small mammals like mice and voles restrict their food foraging until after dark, as they are vulnerable to numerous predators during the day. As a consequence, cats have developed night vision and nocturnal hunting skills. This means that they spend a major part of the daylight hours snoozing, to allow for the alertness needed for their nocturnal forays.

In some circumstances this behaviour may be reversed. For example, Australia is the only continent where reptiles make up a significant proportion of a feral cat's diet. As reptiles need the sun's warmth in order to function and are, therefore, active during the day, the hunting and sleeping timetable of the cats that prey on them is adjusted accordingly.

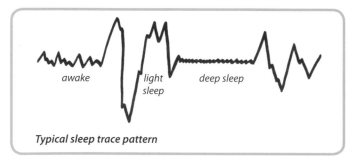

awake | light sleep | deep sleep

Typical sleep trace pattern

Sleep types

Although a cat may snatch a cat nap, when settling down to sleep it goes through a period of about half an hour of light sleep, followed by deep sleep for a shorter period of about seven minutes. During light sleep, the cat can be woken easily. As it moves into deep sleep, the pattern of its brain waves more closely resembles a wakeful state. Unless disturbed, the cat alternates between deep sleep and light sleep. In total, it spends about 30 percent of its sleeping time in deep sleep.

During periods of deep sleep the cat's eyes show rapid eye movements: REM sleep. In us, it is during the deep sleep REM period that we dream, and it seems logical that cats dream during this period, too. Just like us, they twitch – their paws, ears and mouth area may move rhythmically despite the rest of their body being completely relaxed.

The image of the sleeping cat, curled up in front of the fire, is one that we recognize as being a evocative reminder of a cosy home. However, a cat that is comfortably warm will probably stretch out to allow for some heat loss from its body. One that is curled up may be feeling the cold.

A CAT'S LIFE

Posture

The sleeping postures that animals adopt depend very much on their size and body shape, as well as on environmental temperature. Cats share their sleeping postures with other carnivores: they either fold their legs under their body and crouch sphinx-like with their chins down, or lie on their side with their bodies curled around to varying degrees depending on how warm or cold they are.

Cats like to feel confident before sleeping, and nervous cats will often follow their owners around the home for part of the day, and sleep near them. Some cats are fussy in their requirements for cover in the garden before they will attempt to snooze. Just as airing cupboards can be favourite warm sleeping spots inside a house, so a cat will have definite warming and cooling dozing places in the garden. The resident cat will become very upset if another cat usurps its sleeping spots.

related areas...   17   24   25   75

Like us, cats usually yawn widely on waking, but between cats and people, yawning has further significance both as a reassurance signal and, inadvertently, as a greeting. If you walk into a room and approach your cat, which has been cat napping, your sudden appearance can cause it to give a yawn of recognition.

A CAT'S LIFE

Stretching exercises

When your cat wakes up it will give a huge yawn, its mouth fully open and its tongue curled into a ladle shape. It will often stretch its paws out as well. If it then doesn't just settle down for another well-earned snooze, but is actually rising for something important, such as a snack, it will stand tall on long straight legs, pulling itself together while arching its back high, raising and rippling its muscles clearly. It will then move forward, but only to go through the next stage of the waking exercise ritual – the long forward stretch. During this stretch, the cat's rear end stays up and is pushed back while the spine

curves down in an arc towards the front, with the head held low and the front legs and paws extended forwards. The cat then walks and leans forward, with the thoracic spine (mid-backbones) pulling against its back legs, which it stretches out long, as it did with the front paws earlier.

This set of isometric waking warm-up exercises allows the cat to remain in tip-top condition. Through a combination of standing, arching and stretching, it restores flexibility to its spine. This flexibility is of fundamental importance, as not only does it allow the cat to increase its stride length when running, it also allows it to wash and groom itself all over.

related areas... 1 2 22 28

28 Washing

Grooming is important throughout a cat's life. Although we often say that cats just eat and sleep, they have been found to spend between a third and a half of their waking hours in cleaning and tidying their coats and paws. No wonder they become exhausted and have to spend more time sleeping!

How it's done

Cats possess incredibly supple bodies, which allow them to groom nearly all parts of their body easily. With a concerted effort, they can even reach the middle of their backs. The spiny surface of the cat's tongue (see p.16) acts as a very effective comb. Combing inevitably produces loose hairs, some of which a cat swallows, vomiting them up as hairballs later. With some cats, hair causes internal compaction, and these benefit from additional help with their grooming. Grooming can be a problem for cats with long hair, particularly Persians. They have to pull their tongues through each long section of coat for a longer period of time. For modern Persians, daily grooming by their owners is vital.

Temperature control

The cat's tongue also makes an excellent sponge. The papillae on its surface can hold plenty of saliva for grooming. This is also important in temperature control. To avoid having wet fur through sweating, which might cause over-chilling, the cat has sweat glands only in localized areas, such as the pads of the feet. In hot weather, the cat compensates for a lack of sweat glands by using its tongue to spread saliva, which can increase evaporation cooling by up to a third. In cold conditions, the brushing effect of the tongue can also be effective in maintaining body heat – a fluffed-up coat traps a layer of air, which acts as an insulator.

Cleanliness

Grooming is an essential activity to control and reduce infestations of fleas and also enables a cat to spread its own scent around its coat, while at the same time collecting taste information on things with which it has come into contact. When we handle a cat, it will often fussily wash its coat back into place, thereby re-establishing its own scent. The violent washing following mating is, in part, carried out for a similar reason.

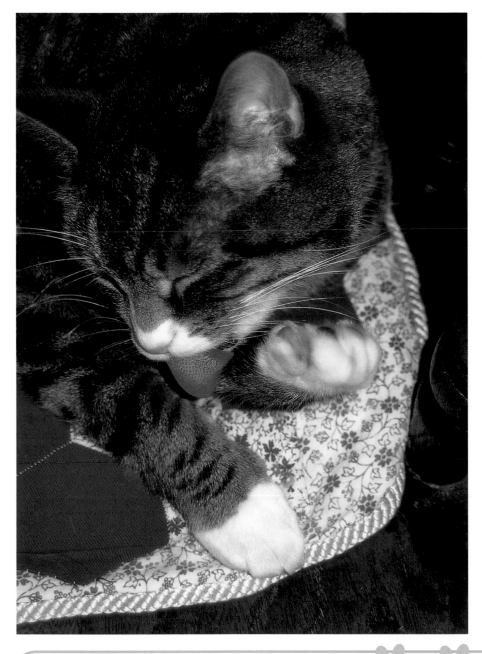

related areas...   31   33   66   81   85

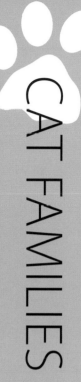

The cat as a symbol of fertility

There has been a long-held association of dog and man, and woman and cat. It may just reflect the historic role of the sexes and the associated role of these animals: men went out hunting with their dogs, while women worked around the homestead where the cat slept beside the fire and stalked mice in the yard. However, 'feline' and 'feminine' are so synonymous that advertisers often use an elegant cat alongside an equally elegant woman to provide a product with a sexy image.

Cat goddesses

Before the rise of Christianity, all the religions across Europe had a mother earth goddess figure who was held as a fount of fertility while being eternally virginal. For the Greeks it was Artemis, for the Romans Diana and the Scandinavians Freyja. The Egyptian goddess Bastet was associated with fertility in women, warmth, love, dance and the moon.

When the Greek Ptolomy became pharaoh, he had inscriptions carved on the cat rock temple near Beni Hasan, and he called the temple 'Speos Artemedos' – Temple of Artemis. Diana was a moon goddess, living in celibacy and presiding over women. When Typhon waged war on the gods, Diana escaped by turning into a cat! In London, St Paul's Cathedral was built on the site of a cult shrine to Diana. A sistrum (ancient wire rattle) excavated in London was used in the worship of the Egyptian fertility goddesses, including

Bastet. It is an intriguing thought that worship of the cat goddess Bastet may have taken place with that of Diana on the site of St Paul's in Roman Londinium.

The importance of Bastet

In Egypt, Bastet was the main cat divinity. Her chief centre of worship was in the city of Bubastis. At the massive annual pilgrimage each year, thousands of devotees, mainly women, sang, danced, drank and shook sistra. The ancient Egyptians noted that the size of the pupil of the cat's eyes varied with the phase of the moon. Although this is just due to the amount of prevailing light, it was thought to be magical. As a woman's fertility cycle has a monthly periodicity, links were recognized between women, cats and the moon.

The cat goddess' fertility role for women is revealed in tomb wall paintings found near Luxor. In scenes of domesticity, husband and wife are portrayed as they hoped to be in their after-lives. When a cat is shown with them, it is always under the seat of the woman. The cat, as an incarnation of the goddess, was positioned to enhance the wife's after-life fertility.

Despite the best endeavours of the Egyptians not only did the reputation of cats leak out of Egypt, but so did some of the animals. Early illustrations of domestic cats in Italy date from around the fourth and fifth centuries BC. However, when Christianity was made the Roman state religion in the fourth century AD, other religions, such as the worshipping of Bastet, were banned. Although the Egyptians' regard for their cats diminished through the passage of time, in Europe, the historic link between cats and women has persisted until the present day.

29 Sex and fertility

The queen has a very distinct cycle of behaviour, linked to her hormone cycle. Shortening day lengths of autumn and winter cause most cats to be anoestrus (sexually inactive). The queen also has sexually quiescent periods between oestrus cycles of activity within the year. These shorter anoestrus periods are called dioestrus.

CAT FAMILIES

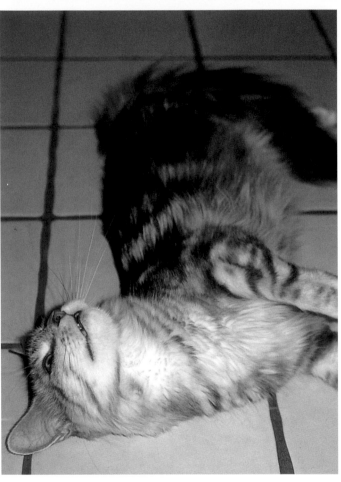

more demonstrative, she will open and close her paws, and she will begin rolling on her back and from side to side. She will also start calling. On entering full oestrus, the queen continues to call and roll, and will also push the back of her head firmly on the ground, thereby leaving sebaceous scents around. The queen is most receptive to male advances on the third to fourth days of oestrus. If she mates, her oestrus ceases within 24 hours under the influence of the progesterone produced from the corpus luteum in the ovaries. However, if she does not mate, she can remain in oestrus for a fortnight, although most noticeably only for around a week.

Without mating, the overall average cycle is about three weeks, but it is very variable, particularly across the pedigree breeds. In Siamese dioestrus is very brief, while some Persians have less frequent oestrus. Siamese queens commonly have long periods of oestrus calling behaviour, which can reach the point where the sound seems almost continuous!

When is a queen ready to mate?

As she goes into pro-oestrus (before full oestrus), the queen starts to become demonstrative and will rub more around objects with her head. Lasting between one and three days, pro-oestrus is typically noted by owners as an increase in their cat's friendliness. During this period a queen may develop a preference for a particular male that courts her by spending time sitting near her. At the same time, some males may try to mate with her but will be rejected – she may clamp down her tail, and possibly strike at them.

As the queen moves towards full oestrus, when her ovaries become ready to ovulate, her movements become progressively

related areas...

30 31 62

30 Courtship

Our medieval ancestors castigated the cat as promiscuous, wanton and wicked based on their observations that cats mate repeatedly over a long period; the queen mates with a number of toms; and queens call out before and during copulation. However, modern studies have revealed that the cat's survival as a species relies on these behaviours.

Preventing inbreeding

Cats are strongly territorial. This favours resident group males in mating and grants social stability, but carries the risk of inbreeding. Cats therefore have a mechanism to avoid this. In most mammals, when an ovum is ripe in an ovary, it is shed spontaneously. However, in cats (and a few other mammals) a triggering device is required to release the egg; the trigger is the penis, which is covered in backward-pointing spines that are longer on more sexually mature toms. Therefore, copulation is needed for ovulation. As the tom withdraws the penis, the raking of the spines inside the queen's vagina stimulates the release of the egg, which occurs 24 hours later. The egg then travels down the fallopian tubes until it reaches the point at which it can be fertilized. And so further copulation is required to fertilize it, which is why the queen allows repeated mating over a long period.

The cat's wild ancestors lived at low densities, separated by territories. The egg takes 24 hours to reach a position at which fertilization is possible, giving time for other toms to reach the receptive queen. Today, with urban feral cats and house cats living at higher densities, even more toms will gather, which has increased genetic diversity still further. It might seem that there is a flaw in this system: if the resident males are displaced by interlopers, why should they support another male's offspring and continue to defend their territory?

The answer is that without genetic flux, the group's survival would be at risk, and consequently, the group male's genetic lineage. Multiple mating allows for multiple fathers in a single litter, although most of the offspring are likely to be those sired by the group's males. At a breeder's cattery, the necessary repeated mating is a disadvantage as the single tom is initially very keen, but repeated matings tire him.

31 Mating

Mating can average around 40 sexual acts in 24 hours and has a repeating cycle. At a breeding establishment where only one tom has access to the queen, there is a relatively prolonged inactive period of 5 to 15 minutes between matings, while both cats rest. Where mating is freer, other males may mate with the queen.

CAT FAMILIES

The mating cycle

Through much of their day-to-day interaction, cats avoid staring at each other. Yet during the mating cycle, queen and tom spend a significant amount of time looking directly at each other. As the tom judges it is time to re-mate he sits up and may make a quiet 'chirrup'. When the queen is ready, she moves forward from her resting position, crawling on lowered front legs and so adopting the lordosis position. Her movement releases a waft of sexual scents, and the readiness of her posture gains his interest. While looking at him, the queen may blink a few times to reassure him. He gives a quiet chirrup request. She may blink some more, and will still look towards him. As he moves in behind her head, he may give another chirrup, before taking an initial hold with his mouth and stepping over her back. The tom's teeth do not usually penetrate the skin, for this is an inhibited grip rather than a bite. Males do not act aggressively but instead solicitously towards the female.

When he mounts the queen, the tom begins a treading movement with his hind legs. At the same time he arches his back, moving towards her vulva to achieve intromission and beginning pelvic thrusts as he does so. The dramatic response of the queen reveals whether intromission has taken place. She growls increasingly louder and then begins to twist her head to one side and then the other. In breeding cattery conditions, full intromission to withdrawal usually takes less than 10 seconds. The tom holds the queen firmly by the neck until almost the last second. In that final moment she will wrench free and threaten or strike at the male with a paw. After washing their urinogenital areas – the queen may also roll on her back several times – both lie on their stomachs forepaws tucked under their chests, resting.

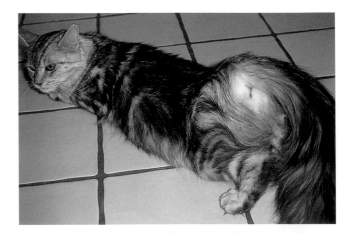

32 Pregnancy

You may suspect that your cat is pregnant when she lavishes more affection on you than usual. Stray (as opposed to fully feral) cats sometimes gravitate back towards people when they are well developed in pregnancy and progesterone levels make them more relaxed.

Preparing for birth

As the queen goes into the last three weeks of her nine-week pregnancy, she will spend more time on her side to relieve the weight of the developing foetuses. She will also try to seek out a suitable nest site as she approaches full term. If she is a house cat, you may offer some deluxe bedding in a cosy cardboard box. However, she may well reject it for a more secluded spot. If this happens, do not be offended: remember that in the cat family males that are not members of her group may kill her kittens. To avoid this (and predators who would take advantage of small helpless kittens when she is away from the nest), she will follow the instincts of her ancestors in finding a secure nesting place. Feral cats may use wiring culverts, the underneath of sheds and temporary buildings, brick piles, timber stacks, old bins and even the wheel arch of a car as nest sites.

The job of rearing the young falls entirely on the female's shoulders. However, in this connection the male is not a waste of space: he is the provider of space. By establishing his large territory, which encompasses hers, he not only ensures that she has an area in which to catch food, but that it is guarded from strange males. Thus in a feral group, the male cats of the queen's group may not provide food directly for the kittens, but they make it available.

Previous offspring

If sub-adults from a previous litter are still around, the pregnant queen is likely to react against them. This will be more apparent in home cats, which, due to indoor heating and lighting, can produce two litters a year. In feral cats this is less likely to occur as they will probably have only one litter per year, just like their wild ancestors. Youngsters from their previous litter will have grown up.

Some cats crave privacy during the birth of their kittens, while others do not seem to mind an audience. Individual births can take only 15 minutes, but there can be gaps of several hours between deliveries. First-time mothers have smaller litters than experienced mothers, regardless of their age.

CAT FAMILIES

Preparation and delivery

As she is about to give birth, the mother-to-be washes herself thoroughly around her mammary glands and genital area to ensure they are clean. She spends more time in the nest, so that the kittens will find it filled with her scent. During labour the queen may well purr, and to ease the kittens' delivery she will sit with one back leg raised. This also enables her to lick away the amniotic sac of each delivered kitten, and it is in this same position that she cleans her genital area between deliveries.

Post delivery

At birth the young are wet and messy, but the mother does not only clean them up as she washes them. She dries the hair of their coats and aligns it; by doing so she is improving the insulating effect of the kittens' coats, which is vital for the warmth and health of their small, unco-ordinated bodies. This grooming process also allows the mother to become familiar with her new brood. (The initial unfamiliarity has allowed instances of 'fooling' the mother into accepting a kitten from another litter, or even

another species.) The mother's washing also stimulates the kitten to take its first breath. She severs the umbilical cord with her teeth, and when the afterbirth is expelled she will eat it for nourishment, enabling her to stay with her kittens for the vital first few days.

If the mother becomes at all anxious over the security of the nest site, she will pick up the kittens individually by the scruff and move them. They stay quiet during this process. In the wild, a move can be dangerous as the kittens are left alone at each end of the journey, while the mother makes successive trips.

related areas... **28** **32** **34**

34 Feeding the kittens

Cats usually make very attentive mothers. In the first four weeks a mother will spend over 90 percent of her time in contact with at least one of her kittens, up to three-quarters of that time in the nest. After this, until weaning at eight weeks, her direct contact gradually reduces to just half of her time.

Suckling

To feed, the mother lies on her side, exposing her four pairs of teats for the kittens to feed on. Although initially happy to lie and suckle, from about three weeks old, the kittens will paddle at their mother to stimulate more milk flow. In litters up to the number of teat pairs – up to four kittens – the new born are usually of comparable weight. With bigger litters, the average birth weight is lower; the mother makes more milk, but the supply is not infinite, so the average weight of the kittens remains less than those from smaller litters.

Kittens have been shown to demonstrate some nipple preference within a few days of being born. One litter was seen to have developed a remarkable degree of loyalty to feeding position within a few hours of birth, and this did not become more random as the weeks of

suckling progressed. A major advantage for cats in having position loyalty is to avoid teat laceration by sharp claws. Additionally the kitten may be displaying a form of territoriality. It is possible that the prime position is the pair of teats near the mother's head, where caring licking is also on offer, along with visual cue reinforcement from the mother's face. The furthest place from the mother's head may be the least favoured.

First solids

During the transition to solid food, a feral mother has to spend a significant time hunting for prey to bring back to the kittens. She does not receive direct hunting support from the male and so has to leave the kittens in a safe lair. Rearing her young alone means her kittens are focused on her actions for their survival.

Consequently, if she gives an alarm growl, they will instantly stop their play and dive under the nearest cover.

related areas... 17 20 22 38 40

Growing up fast!

It is impossible not to fall in love with a little kitten. The reason for this is that as well as looking small, fluffy and cute, they have a flatter face with proportionately bigger eyes than their parents. This appeals to us, for they are the features of our own babies. Cute though kittens are, their extreme vulnerability when born is fairly soon left behind. Within seven weeks, they will be weaned and have begun to develop the sensory control that they will need for hunting and protection.

CAT FAMILIES

Birth to 3 weeks

When kittens are born their eyes are tight shut and remain so for up to 10 days. For the first few days, they have little hearing, but do have a reasonable sense of smell. Combined with the sense of touch, which they develop while in the womb, their ability to smell and sense warmth allows them to find their mother's teats. New-born kittens lack the strength to lift their bodies off the ground. Their small round heads lie flat on the floor on their chins virtually all of the time when they are not suckling. They exhaust quickly and it is an effort for them to haul themselves up onto a teat. A 'rooting reflex' means they automatically push their heads into warm places.

By the time the kittens are a week old, their prolonged feeding – up to eight hours at a time – will have had a noticeable effect. Their bodies are much fuller and more rounded as they have been gaining weight rapidly. Although their tummies are still on the ground, their limbs have more strength and they can keep their heads up,

new born kittens

but they still spend a lot of time sleeping. Their ears are very small, but their eyes are less tightly sealed, and a gap of eye can often be seen in the corners nearest the nose. Their appreciation of what is bright and what is dark will be improving. When the mother leaves the kittens, they usually remain huddled together, like a pile of sausages. If one does move out, it soon moves back towards the group, but on extremely shaky limbs, its body rocking back and forth as it moves slowly along.

At two weeks old, the kittens' eyes are open but they are very cloudy, with

little ability to bring the world into proper focus. When not with their mother, the kittens still prefer to spend time huddled as a warm group. The mother spends a considerable amount of time washing and grooming her kittens. Part of this is so they roll over or get up and so allow her to stimulate them to eliminate; she then licks away the droppings, which would otherwise foul the nest. The kittens' progress is still made on their tummies with wobbly legs pushing them along, but a week makes quite a difference. They clamber more readily across each other and are more venturesome, moving with heads bobbing but still held very low. They continue to gain weight rapidly, but although their ears are growing they are still buckled down. It is also at this stage that some kittens begin to place their paws beside their mother's teats, but as yet they do not have the power to paddle. The kittens are beginning to look cute at three weeks, rather than just like blobs. Their ears are firmer and more upright, but still with a bit of a downward curve. They

one week   *two weeks*   *three weeks*   *four weeks*

have begun to discover walking, although their tummies do not leave the ground by much. The experience is still new to them and their paw control is very shaky. Their heads, bodies and tails are still held low, with their back legs pushing along. However, they will now look directly at you, although they still stay close to mother. As the kittens are filling out in size, the point has come when suckling becomes a tight fit! They are strong enough to paddle at the teat to stimulate milk flow.

4 to 5 weeks

At four weeks the kittens' ears are properly upright. They can walk about with their tummies well off the ground, although they are not yet fully upright. However, they can and do experiment at standing tall on their legs from time to time. They now often hold their tails upright, where previously this had not really been possible. With their greater mobility, the kittens are becoming much more adventurous. Their sight has become clearer, which is an advantage for their increasing play with litter mates.

The kittens suddenly become much more lively and mobile after about five weeks. They will focus on and pursue play objects and will even clamber up things, including people if they are sitting down. Their eyes look crystal clear, and their hearing is now fully developed. This increase in the function of their senses has coincided with their increased ability to move about.

They seem to be always on the go, but then they will suddenly nose dive and take a nap. They try out their teeth by gnawing on baskets and just about anything else, and have certainly developed the cats' curiosity to find out what is behind things. Their play is becoming more vigorous, with batting occurring. At the same time, their mother is cutting down on stimulating elimination and licking away the excreta as the kittens are more capable of eliminating for themselves.

6 weeks

At six weeks, the kittens have now undeniably entered their cutest phase, with perked ears and adorable faces. Their senses are really attuned and they are walking about fully upright on their legs. The amount of time they spend playing with objects increases hugely – roll a ping-pong ball gently towards them and they will investigate and bat it. If their mother is bringing in prey from the outside world, they will be keen to grip it and will growl in possession. If you play with toys of similar size or with a cord, they will grasp that in their mouths and will show a determination to pull! They can be seen playing gently with their mother's tail, or with their own or those of their litter mates.

By this age the kittens are becoming more self-contained, in as much as they will not only initiate play with a dangling string, but will also sit quietly between some activities. Climbing has become one of their major preoccupations. The mother

cat will have started cutting down on suckling and she sometimes sits upright to discourage the kittens to continue.

Weaning and young adulthood

Weaning is usually accomplished by the time the kittens are seven weeks old. As they have been growing, so have their food requirements, in part at the expense of the mother, who will have been losing nearly 6g (¼oz) a day in weight during the lactation period.

eight weeks

By eight weeks old, the responses of the kittens are becoming more mature. By the time they are ten weeks old, although they are still smaller and slimmer, their proportions and posture are virtually those of an adult. From nine weeks on their play becomes more earnest, until around 14 weeks of age its aggressive edge loosens litterhood ties. The kittens are now ready to become independent juvenile cats.

five weeks   *six weeks*   *seven weeks*

35 Sexing kittens

When you are looking for a kitten for your household, it is fairly important to know the sex of the ones you look at. Unless you are obtaining your kitten from an experienced breeder, don't rely on what the existing owner judges the sex to be. It is not at all uncommon for Tom to have to be changed to Tabitha on discovery that the identification was a bit slack!

How to tell them apart

Although behavioural characteristics will soon tell you the sex of an adult cat – if you can't spot the differences from behind – kittens are more difficult because they are not fully developed. However, the basic rule is that when you look at the rear end of a kitten the apertures of the vulva and anus are close together in the female. In the male, the apertures, this time of the penis and the anus, are further apart to allow for the position of the testes. If you have any doubts as to what 'close' and 'further apart' mean, the Abyssinian kitten with its mother (left) is male, while in the group (below) the central kitten is female.

related areas...　　　　19　29　73

Mother cats are renowned for their caring devotion to their kittens and most of the time disagreements between littermates are rare and shortlived. Sometimes things can go awry, but fortunately it is unusual. However, if you are expecting a litter, it is as well to be aware of the possibility.

CAT FAMILIES

Bullying

An example of a problem occurred in a young litter that I monitored. The mother cat showed due attentiveness to her kittens, fed and washed them all appropriately, and attended to them if they called out during the early weeks of kittenhood. It was a hot summer, and as they grew towards weaning she would lie away from them to cool off. However, at this stage her attentions towards the smallest black kitten became over-zealous. She would hold him around the neck with her paws, biting and kicking him – actions sufficiently violent to cause him to cry out. This behaviour was in complete contrast to that she displayed towards all her other kittens, although she did continue to wash and suckle the black kitten along with the rest of the litter.

By the time he was weaning, yet still taking milk from his mother, the little kitten was noticeably more fearful than the others. Although all the kittens had been handled regularly since they were very young, a finger proffered towards the black kitten provoked a defensive hiss. In contrast, his slightly larger brothers and sisters would move forward to investigate the finger. At this point, a transformation occurred in the relationship between this kitten and some of his littermates. While play between all of them was becoming naturally more vigorous, the fearful black kitten began to be attacked more determinedly and for prolonged periods by other kittens. Its mother's actions seemed to have made it more nervous, which in turn made it a 'victim' for its littermates. Such early conditioned behaviour is usually hard to break in later life.

related areas... **37** **40** **48** **49**

37 Imprinting

Once young kittens' eyes begin opening and they start to move about, they begin to encounter other animals around the nest area that have been tolerated by the mother. These are happily accepted as littermates by the kittens, for the mother would fiercely exclude everything else.

Meeting people

Whatever they are (including possible prey), the kittens will accept these tolerated animals, an acceptance that continues into adulthood. When kittens are brought up with non-cat species, such as puppies, the kittens show a similar distress when those animals are taken away as when a feline littermate is removed.

If we wish our cats to behave towards us as if we were littermates, rather than the enormous alien species we are, it is vital that kittens are habituated to people during the period of time when they learn to recognize littermates. Eileen Karsh established that the sensitive period for habituating kittens to people is from two weeks to seven weeks. Cats handled regularly at this time were prepared when older to stay on someone's lap longer and approached people more readily. Cats that were handled after this period, that is from weaning onwards, behaved no differently to cats that had not been handled at all. Unfortunately, this corresponds with the very time, post-weaning, when kittens are normally taken to their new homes from catteries or rescue centres. All too often, as young kittens they will not have been handled regularly. Brought into new homes where they are the focus of attention, they receive a lot of handling, yet it seems this will not socialize them as well as a little time spent each day before weaning. Consequently, as adult cats they will not relate to people as well as they might otherwise have done.

Bonding

The problem is that it would be traumatic to remove kittens before weaning to their new homes so that their new owners could relate to them, for this deprives them of their mother's attention and makes them overly dependent. Karsh found that it was not necessary for the habituators to be the eventual owners: they just need to be people. However, kittens do bond with particular people, so the ideal is to spend some time, regularly, well before weaning at the cattery with the kitten you have chosen. This should be in the nest area in the presence of the mother, who must be trusting.

related areas... 60 61 67 78 79 80

38 Weaning

Weaning is the transition from milk to solid food for the developing young and in cats is usually accomplished by the time they are seven weeks old. In part, the mother starts to wean them because she needs to rebuild her own strength. At this stage, the kittens gradually become less able to digest the lactose in milk.

Cutting down

Over a period of days, the mother gradually becomes less willing to provide the kittens with milk and once they have reached a certain weight, her inability to keep up with demand for milk forces the change in her behaviour. The larger the litter, the earlier she will begin to cut down on the kittens' accessibility to suckling, either by moving, such as sitting upright during feeding, or by lying on her nipples. This doesn't always prevent an enterprising kitten pushing in.

Post-weaned Kittens

At seven or eight weeks old kittens in domestic litters are ready to go to their new homes. They will be eating solids and should be more or less fully weaned.

related areas... 34 39 65

When the kittens are four to five weeks old, if she has access to the outside world, the mother cat will start to bring in dead prey for them. Up to this point, in the isolated security of the mother's nest area, the kittens are unlikely to have met other animals, dead or alive, or any food source other than milk from their mother.

CAT FAMILIES

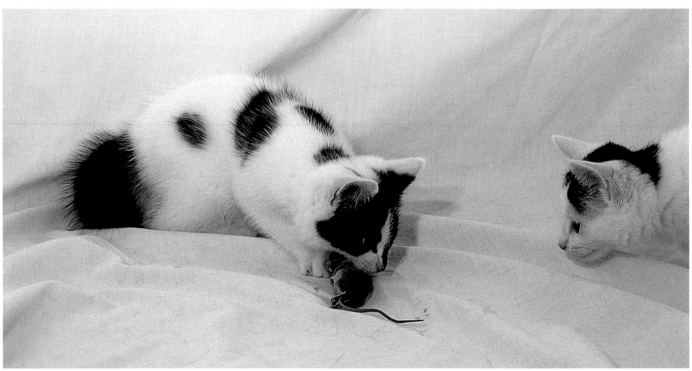

Introducing prey

Initially, when she begins to bring prey to the nest, the mother will growl and keep the prey. She is not yet an instructor. Instead, she portrays herself as an apparent competitor, which stimulates the kittens' interest. However, she avoids frightening them by intermingling her growls with encouraging purrs.

Kittens need to learn that food is contained within dead prey. The introduction to prey in the rough and tumble of the nest makes it more likely that they will realize this, especially with soft-bodied, small prey such as voles or mice, where play and seizure often puncture the skin and so enable a connection with food to be made.

Progressive teaching

By the time the kittens are nine weeks old, their mother will be bringing live prey back to the nest (although she may kill it before a kitten takes possession). Her progressive training of her kittens from introducing them first to dead prey then increasingly lively

prey ensures that they become more expert at dealing with it. She brings prey primarily for consumption, but is also able to display the technique of killing it. Some isolated kittens manage to kill without these demonstrations, but those that are able to watch their mothers are more successful in their own hunting.

A transforming experience

Observations I made confirm that the first meeting of a kitten with dead prey brings about a transformation in behaviour. From mild interest and kittenish reactions, the four-and-a-half week old kitten suddenly became alert and focused when the dead prey was lightly tugged in front of it. It held it with its jaws and began growling repeatedly in a possessive manner. The kitten then sniffed its prey – a dead mouse. At first it did not follow the mouse when it was pulled away, but sniffed the area where it had been. However after a few seconds it began to mouth the prey, then, when the prey was repeatedly pulled away, its response became more serious and it soon made its first bite, a correctly orientated nape bite.

40 Kitten play

Kittens start playing when they have developed mobility and co-ordination. Although earlier attempts will be made, it is usually around about five to six weeks old that they can leap and climb easily, with a playful zest for movement. They now have good paw-to-mouth co-ordination, which enables them to play with and grip dangling string.

Specific moves

Early cumbersome movements develop into play fighting, then as weaning approaches play hunting moves are seen. These are classified in one system as 'mouse pounces', 'bird swats' and 'fish scoops', but a problem with connecting kitten play with adult behaviours is that more than one behaviour can relate to a kitten movement. The 'bird swat', for example, is used extensively in the recapturing of birds, and is also that of standing defence. Similarly, the 'fish scoop', which is not as frequent a play move as the bird swat (but is particularly feline), allows the cat to reach into holes and spaces and root around for prey (see also pp.38–9).

An alternative classification (which does not make a link with adult use) describes kitten behaviour in such terms as 'scoop', 'grasp', 'poke' and 'mouth'. When kittens interact socially with each other their positions have been classified as 'chase', 'vertical stance', 'belly up', 'pounce' and so on. Each of the moves used on objects is also used in social moves with other kittens. One kitten will bat another or make a scoop move at a tail. Similarly, social moves like pounce and chase can be used on a small ball.

These moves can be likened to adult behaviour. For example, if one kitten is standing up on its back legs, the responding kitten will go down on its back, and vice versa, in moves similar to those of a fight. In addition, kittens engage in more object play than by less obligate carnivores, so a fair part of this is linked to adult predatory behaviour. John Bradshaw has made the observation that object play, although compared to hunting, is most comparable to post-capture 'play'.

Play and hierarchy

Kittens' moves are signalled as play by their exaggeration and lack of aggressive intent or intensity, which means bites are inhibited. Although littermate play around weaning usually lacks the aggression that can appear in older kitten play, there are weight and confidence differences between kittens. Within the nest area, a litter hierarchy develops. The nervous behaviour of underweight kittens can evoke more forthright responses from heavier kittens. As kittens are weaned around 7–8 weeks of age their games change to incorporate more object play and they become more focused on both predatory and combative play. This becomes increasingly more boisterous until by 14–16 weeks old, growing aggression is weakening the youthful bonds.

CAT BEHAVIOUR

Social structure in feral cats

I have a long-standing interest in feral cats and began my detailed study of them in the mid-1970s, a time when they were poorly understood and colonies were considered to be 'loose assemblages' with no social structure. My main study group was in Fitzroy Square, London W1. The colony had a number of dedicated feeders and the site was ideal for the cats, with protective railings, a large mature garden with good cover, yet also with open grass and sunning spots.

Long-term group

It soon became clear that this was no random, varying aggregation of cats. On the contrary, I observed that the same animals held the site day after day, and, as the study went on, year after year. The group had been in continuous residence for 20 years, and probably much longer.

At this time it was assumed that life for a feral was nasty, brutish – and short. But I discovered that most were fit and robust. I weighed my study groups and found their weights were comparable to house cats. A conflicting assumption was that feral living made cats huge, so I also

measured them. Again the similarities with house cats were more noticeable than the differences.

Other fascinating information came to light through my studies. For example, I found the ranges of my colonies were smaller than those of the dockyard feral groups studied by Jane Dards in Portsmouth, and much smaller than those farmyard cats monitored by David MacDonald and Peter Apps. Yet, remarkably, the pattern was the same: toms ranged wider than queens, using about 10 times the area, and the groups clumped around a source of food. I realized that more food resulted in more

cats, for with more food available the cats do not have to travel so widely to find it and therefore their ranges are smaller.

Until we started to log the cats' movements, no one really knew how the cats' social system of land use worked. Similar studies of tigers and forest wildcats have shown a cat family pattern of males holding significantly larger ranges than females. But, while the ranges of female tigers and forest wildcats do not overlap much, the English feral cat studies showed the cats clumped around a core area that included a major food source, like a feeder, or rabbit warren. Where food is more distributed, queen's ranges do not overlap so much. So feral domestic cats have flexibility over their ranges, which allows them to tolerate other cats if there is a good local source of food. Yet, at the same time, they have the same basic pattern as the rest of the cat family.

Around the world

I have studied cats living feral around the world, and found that they live remarkably similar lives despite radically different environmental conditions. In rural areas, food availability is insufficient to sustain large numbers of cats, so densities are low; the reverse is true in towns. In addition, a significant part of the cat population is always in a feral state. In the ancient bazaars of Egypt there are some feral cats whose lineage contains few ancestors that have known domestic life; remarkably, this is almost equally true in Britain.

In Britain, pet cats claim most of the country's extensive suburban landscape. To obtain food our house cats only have to stagger from their snoozing spots to their food bowls. Consequently, feral cats cannot achieve the same density of numbers as nearby house cats, and require larger areas in which to scavenge for food. The ferals live in the gaps left by the house cats in the suburban landscape, such as hospital grounds, factories and squares. In many other countries, house cats are

less common, and lead wilder lives, at lower densities, like farm cats. The nearer a rural economy approaches subsistence agriculture, the more the cat remains a working animal. In a village in the Spanish Pyrenees, I talked to a lady about her cats. Her kitchen was the main room of the house and chickens scratched around its floor. Her cats were rodent controllers. She threw them chunks of meat, over which they growled at each other. I have met the same situation in many other parts of the world.

Feral control

The control of feral cats is an emotive issue. It is clear that killing all cats in a colony is not successful, for eradication is rarely

total, and cats move in from other areas. A controlled, stable existing colony prevents this 'vacuum effect'. If a colony is neutered and returned to its area, it will continue to hold the location and keep out other cats by its presence. The group's population will gradually decline over a few years.

In the early 1970s ex-model and feral cat carer Celia Hammond became dissatisfied with the ineffective 'trap and kill' approach and began to put neutered cats back on sites. When I monitored my Fitzroy Square cats, before and after neutering I found that the reducing population continued to hold their area for many years. The Cat Action Trust, which I launched, has gone on to neuter many thousands of cats all across Britain. Subsequently, the practice of neutering and returning feral cats back to their site has been applied widely by organizations around the world.

Although many organizations and individual feeders in the USA have been using this technique to control feral populations, it is not without its opponents, some of whom, regardless of appearances to the contrary, believe these cats must be leading a terrible life and consider that it is best to 'save' them from suffering by killing them. In a huge cat owning society opinions are bound to vary, but discussing differences is leading to a better understanding of not only the neuter-and-return method, but also of the feral-living cat.

41 Making friends

Carnivores that hunt in packs, such as dogs, have to work within a hierarchy. Ranking squabbles can lead to dangerous confrontations, so pack hunters possess a repertoire of appeasement behaviours. In contrast, cats are intensely territorial and hunt as individuals, and the ways in which they deal with social interaction and aggression are very different.

CAT BEHAVIOUR

Appeasement behaviour

Before domestication, solitary hunting cats could not reach high densities due to the lack of food sources, so there was little need for appeasement behaviours. Even today, cats prefer to threaten, fight, withdraw or avoid. When domestic cat groups come together, it is for social activities. When they are held together by the accessibility of food, they show tolerance rather than co-operation. As a cat's survival is not dependent on a pack, there is no need to establish rank, and so aggression in a group is not so critical, neither is appeasement. However, the group does bond using activities such as

rubbing and mutual grooming, as well as having distance tolerance; as owners, we equate these with affection. Yet the strategy cats employ of being territorial, and delineating territory by a system of scent and other marks, is a form of sabre-rattling in absence. Declaring presence in this way is certainly not appeasement but it does avoid aggressive interactions, unless the intruder ignores them.

In observations of free-ranging farm cats, where contact occurred between cats 93 percent were bonding moves (mutual licking and rubbing), while only 7 percent were aggressive. In farm and feral cats aggression between group cats is mild, and only serious towards intruding males. In suburban house cats and confined cats aggression is more frequent due to the

density of the population itself, and when this closeness has not allowed time or inclination for contact permission signals.

Friends?

Cats do not normally sit close together unless they are group or family members. In households with more than one cat, the dynamics of the social relationships between the cats can be up and down. A measure of how good the relationship is at any time is how close and how frequently your cats curl up and snooze together. Yawning and blinking are also bonding signals. Even confined cats will maintain their distances from each other if they do not believe they are a group.

42 Adult play

We recognize cat play when we see it, and know that it is more common in juvenile cats than in adults. It seems to be practice for life-skills development, yet it has been harder to evaluate than other behaviours, such as predation. That is partly a comment on our relative perspective, but it is also true that predation is less ambiguous than play.

What is playing?

Play is most recognizable in species like the cat, whose full range of behaviour is not present immediately after birth and who have complex nervous systems. Play has been called paradoxical behaviour, in that it often causes the reverse of the non-play behaviour sequence it mirrors. For example, a successful adult territorial fight will cause the opponent to withdraw, while kitten fighting play is part of the socializing between littermates.

Much of what is commonly termed 'playing with prey' is not play but the inhibited form of dispatching prey (see p.36). However, when such sequences are prolonged in house cats, it can seem as if playfulness has been incorporated. When hunting moves are made by a cat against inanimate objects, such as a ball of paper, the component of play is easier to identify. This is particularly so if the cat initiates the event.

Playing with people

When adult cats play with us, it is usually considered to be retention of juvenile character due to our size and support. One factor that is often overlooked is that our care of house cats gives them significantly more free time. They do not have to catch prey to survive, nor do they have to patrol huge territories. The drives for these behaviours are nonetheless present and will surface as play. Although adult cats play less than kittens, they will play by themselves, not always requiring our presence for stimulation. So comparisons between kitten rates of play and those of a solitary house cat are not fair, for a good proportion of kitten chase and pounce moves involve the other kittens in the litter. A fairer comparison would be with adult cats playing with us.

43 Making faces

Cats' faces reflect their mood, but although they indicate this to other cats, the changes are primarily to give a functional advantage to the cat. When the cats' eyes widen they gain wider peripheral vision, an advantage when anticipating being attacked. When the eyes narrow they gain better depth perspective, an advantage in judging where to attack.

CAT BEHAVIOUR

Ear positions

When a cat fluffs up its tail in a dramatic way, and arches its back, it may be defensive or aggressive. Cats involved in a stand-off will be making 'mrrow' threatening sounds, but to read what is actually happening look at their ears. If these are down flat against their head, the cat is the defender. If they are down flat but with a twist so that the tips of the back of the ear can be seen from the front, then that cat is the aggressor. These positions can seem very similar to us, but there is no such ambiguity for the cats. Territorial confidence will usually give one cat the advantage over another, and there will be

an aggressor and a defender. However, two large, equally confident males both flagging aggression is the sign for a relatively rare, but very serious dispute (see pp.78–9).

If a fight develops, the defender's ears will remain flat throughout, but the aggressor's get folded flat with a flick at the instant it dives onto the other cat. If it remains the clear aggressor, as it disengages the ears will lift quickly back into the aggressive position. However, if it is not intending to continue the aggression, the ears return to neutral. These ear position flips happen so fast that it is almost impossible to register them clearly at normal speed.

Eye shapes

The defending cat's pupils will be wide open with fear, while the aggressor's will be narrowed tight. At such times, this is part of the 'fight or flight' reaction of the cat's sympathetic autonomic nervous system, which also causes its hair to stand on end. The aggressor threatens with its posture by approaching sideways-on to look larger, and its head turns as it gets ready to throw itself onto the other cat. The frightened defending cat will either crouch down, prepared to strike, or go down on its back, ready to use its back legs to rake the underside of the aggressor as it attacks.

Ear signals

Adult cats may use their ears to signal mood to other adults and as an indication of aggression or defence. Young kittens have little control over their ears. In kittenhood, an attack is usually just a play attack, and even when they can position their ears to express threat or defence, they rarely do so.

CAT BEHAVIOUR

Ear mobility

I believe kittens recognize that at this stage in their life a threat is not real, and so a real adult response need not be made. Part of the reason for not positioning their ears in an aggressive or defensive manner, however, is physical: during early development kittens cannot make such signals due to the immobility of their ears.

New born to one week – ears are round and immobile.

Two weeks – ears are developing but bent over all the time and still immobile, and in consequence look permanently defensive.

Three weeks – ears have become erect, but are fat and devoid of much movement.

Four weeks – ears are fully upright.

Five weeks – ears are increasingly flexible, allowing them to flatten but still not to fold properly at the back.

Six weeks – ears are big and can fold on contact with something.

Seven weeks – ears can now fold properly, but in the mayhem of continuous play kittens do not normally give aggressive ear signals.

related areas...   40   43   45   47

45 Tail play

Throughout their lives cats seem to experience an occasional fascination with their tail. Even though it has been there since birth, they will suddenly seem to notice it following behind them and begin to chase and grab at it. Tail play is amusing for onlookers and appears to be just that – play.

CAT BEHAVIOUR

Your tail or mine?

First seen at five weeks, by seven weeks of age tail play is a real pull on kitten attention! Typically, a kitten will begin making patting movements, following the tail of a littermate. The littermate, though, may be busy with some other play action and not react. After a few seconds of tail following, the first kitten's attention is usually drawn to something else and the game ends. It may be that tail following is hierarchical, for some kittens seem to be more tail-followers, while others are more tail-followed.

Older adult house cats also engage in tail play. A game that is often quoted by owners as an example of their cats 'having a sense of humour'. Often the cat will set itself up for a period of self-motivated play by getting up onto a sofa-back or staircase post and curving itself around, with its head down and foreleg extended downwards. Once in position, it will friskily attempt to grab hold of its own tail. This behaviour frequently takes place when the cat is in a heightened mood, perhaps because its owner has just returned home. Owners will often collaboratively play with their cat in this heightened state, by touching its back or putting something, such as a pencil or piece of string, where the cat can grab at it.

related areas...   40   44   46

Tail signals

The cat's tail has great flexibility, which enables it to provide balance, not only in fast cornering moves and climbing, but for position compensation, such as when a cat is eliminating. Tail positions and movements are also expressions of a cat's moods and may be used in social relationships.

Bonding or appeasement?

When is a gesture one of social bonding and when a matter of appeasement? In essence, appeasement aims to prevent an act of aggression and is carried out by an animal of lesser rank. Rank in cats is not particularly clear cut, so close interactive moves are more likely to be social. So whereas in dogs tails are used to warn off aggression or indicate submissiveness, in cats tail raising may be a 'request' to allow contact rubbing, such mutual co-operation being motivated by the need to bond rather than to appease. It is possible to recognize an 'acknowledgement hierarchy', as the affectionate move of rubbing may be initiated more frequently by a 'low ranking' cat towards a 'high ranking' one than the other way round. I believe that tail-up is not just a permission to rub, but also constitutes a greeting, allowing cats to come closer amicably.

Tail language

Upright, with tip curved over – the cat in 'neutral', with the tail tip turning back and forth in time with the walk.

Erect for its full length – the greeting to another cat or ourselves, often followed by rubbing. When kittens greet their mother, particularly when she has prey, they will raise their tails and rub along her asking for food. When we rub along our cat's back the tail will flick up into this position. If stroking is continued along the back, some cats will fluff up the lower third of their tail, and curve the rest as they paddle and purr. The involvement of anal scent glands can be detected. When the cat is lying out full length with tail erect it is trying to cool down.

Erect for full length, quivering – the position adopted for spraying, with the cat's hind legs standing tall. This also occurs with 'air spraying', whereby neutered cats make the movements of spraying without actually doing so, when they go into an area where they are not fully confident.

Held to one side – during the female sexual position (lordosis), to allow mounting.

Tail flicks of seated cat – used to check that nothing is behind it. When we are behind a cat, it will thump its tail repeatedly against us. At times this indicates irritation.

Tail wagging – this ranges from small irritated flicks, which may express emotional conflict or a cat torn between intentions, to its most pronounced form between male cats preparing for a fight, accompanied by growling.

Tail held down, with elevated rump – when an aggressive cat stands side-on to another cat.

Fluffed up, arched tail – when a cat arches its back and wavers between being aggressive and defensive. Young cats in particular behave like this towards dogs. The same fluffed tail, but positioned straight out or down, is seen when the balance has tilted towards aggression.

Tail down wrapped against body – occurs when a contented cat is lying in comfortable conditions. However, in an intimidated cat this is normally a defensive (but not submissive) posture.

Tail vertical in air, cat on its back – the ultimate defensive posture of the cat, protecting the nape of the neck and ready to kick the opponent. It normally follows from the previous position.

related areas... **43** **47** **51**

47

The witches' cat

Most cat owners are familiar with the impressive and distinctive witches' cat posture, by which a cat makes itself appear far bigger than it is. From studies made of cat postures and expressions in various threatening situations, it would seem that this is a mid-point of arousal, both defensive and aggressive.

Standing its ground

Detailed observations of cats suggest that their body postures and facial expressions do not just go from the aggressive threat/ attack to the low crouch of standing defence. The witches' cat is the middle ground, where the cat stands high on its legs, with its back fixed in a high arch and its tail and back bristling with fur. This is the pose that inexperienced juvenile cats adopt when faced with an apparent threat; kittens learn it early in their development. The cat also stands side-on to the threat to maximize the visual image it presents.

The witches' cat is often used against dogs. The posture is a mixture of defence and attack – it has the high legs of the aggressive cat but the pulled-down head, bristling fur and hissing of the defensive cat. A defensive cat trying to be aggressive will bravely stand its ground using this posture. Its walking movements will be wooden, due to the conflict within the cat. Its eyes too will be midway between fearful pupil dilation and aggressive closure.

related areas...   **43**   **44**   **46**   **48**   **50**

48 Scaredy cat

In adult cats there are two clear patterns of nervous, unsettled behaviour – the timid cats and the dependent cats. However, this distinction is only noticeable in connection with their owners; when the owner is absent, the dependent cat's wariness may seem little different to a completely timid cat that is not socialized to anyone.

Effects of timidity

Timid cats are vulnerable to stress, and some of their characteristics are induced by that stress. They can be generally very wary of people, disturbance and noise, and will seek out refuges and avoid social contact. They do not readily explore if placed in new surroundings, instead often sitting still, stressed and nervous. They generally run sooner from strangers than do more confident cats. Eileen Karsh found that there may be a genetic predisposition to timidity in some cats, but that handling early in their lives produces better socialization in most cats, and as a consequence less timidity in adulthood.

To find a measure of timidity, and how people affect such cats, Karsh timed how long cats took to come out of a compartment to investigate. When no one was about, confident cats wandered out within 18 seconds, but if a person was there they came right out in 3 seconds. In contrast, timid cats took 86 seconds with no one about, and nearly the same, at 75 seconds, if someone was there.

Timidity in otherwise confident cats

I found the effect of not only the lack of early kittenhood habituation but also the lack of adult human social interaction to be quite dramatic when free-ranging feral cats were taken into captivity and placed in a confined space the size of a small room. When a person walked nearby, some of the cats crammed themselves into the narrow gap behind the door. These were timid cats in the sense of not having been habituated to people, but in their normal activities they were competent and capable.

Similarly, among house cats there are many territorially confident males, with larger ranges than the local average, that are avid, successful hunters and trusting of their owners, but which rapidly 'evaporate' if strangers are about. There is therefore a distinction between timidity in response to people from lack of habituation during kittenhood and later life, and general timidity.

related areas... 37 49 88

49 Clingy cat

Nervous, dependent cats are the 'one-man dogs' of the cat world, keeping a dependent fixation upon their owners, yet remaining very shy of other people in general and exhibiting 'nervy' behaviour. Within a family they can gradually broaden their acceptance of close people.

CAT BEHAVIOUR

What causes dependency?

Kittens stand a higher chance of growing into nervous, dependent cats if they were small in size in relation to the litter average, were taken from their mother too early before being fully weaned, and were not properly habituated to people during their early weeks of life. Kittens handled by more than one person are more accepting of strangers in later life than those handled by only one person.

Recognizing dependency

Nervous, dependent cats will sit on your lap more frequently, spend more time in your presence, knead you more with chest paddling, and rub near you or on nearby objects more frequently than most cats. Due to the confidence gained by your arrival they will want to rub, but because of their anxious lack of confidence they will mainly rub on objects near you. These moves are the equivalent of 'air-kisses' in

people! The nervous, dependent cat is also prone to behaving in a depressed manner. When put in a cattery, it may refuse to eat and so lose weight, for in this situation it is deprived of you, its focus, as well as its home.

Female dependency

Nervous, dependent female cats can exhibit an apparently strange piece of behaviour, even in response to their owners, when they are flustered and anxious. A hand run down their backs in a normal gentle stroking manner can cause them to lower their backs as they walk. If the hand is lowered, they further lower their hindquarters in the manner of a limbo-dancer. However, once such an animal is reassured, her anxiety will instantly melt and she will not only stand to be stroked but will raise her rump firmly and rub around her owner's hand. Such cats have been parodied as a 'neurotic mess', flipping back and forth between nervous retreat and anxious clinging. They produce this and other ambivalent behaviours due to their conflict between wanting to make contact and at the same time fearing it. They may run to the catflap as if fearful, but return as fast if called, then retreat at any movement, only to return once more when their owner calls again in exasperation.

50 Territorial disputes

While cats can live in reasonably close proximity quite happily and with only the occasional disagreement, territorial disputes can arise even among house cats, especially when a newcomer arrives in the area. For some cats such disputes can have a devastating effect upon their confidence for a prolonged period.

Multi-cat households

Outside territorial events can also affect the relationships within a multi-cat household. My own neuter tom Leroy was housebound, recovering from an abscess following an attack by a new neighbouring tom. During this period, and for a while afterwards, his confidence was not what it had been, and my other cat Tabitha took advantage of the situation and asserted herself, initiating mild aggression. Cats added to an existing multi-cat household may have difficulty adjusting; some not feeling secure may even leave or become aggressive. Burmese are commonly reported as having low-key spats.

related areas... 17 18 19 43 48 49 51

Scrapping

For those who have not kept cats before, some aspects of a cat's aggression can come as a surprise. Once hierarchies are established among dogs, it is not common for dogs to attack bitches. For cats, though, territory is more important than hierarchy, so male-female battles will occur. However, the torn ears of the wide-ranging, intact tom testify to its more frequent and serious fights with other males.

Surprise spats

Owners may become concerned when cats that generally get on well suddenly have a spat. One cat can be apparently minding its own business snoozing, when the other cat attacks it, seemingly without provocation. In reality, this will not often come as too much of a surprise to the attacked cat, for despite its appearance it will usually have had its eyes open a little and been aware of the other cat's approach. Indeed, its wariness may be partly responsible for inducing the attack.

It is usual for the defending cat to intercept an attack by rolling on its back and raising its front paws, while its ears flatten instantaneously to protect them. While staying on its back, the defending cat will try to take the weight of the attacker with its back paws and kick to shift it. At the same time, it will initially hold the attacking cat with its front paws; then, using alternate paws with claws protruding, it may bat rapidly at the head of the aggressor until the aggressor withdraws from immediate contact, the defending cat's claws flashing back and forth in front of its nose.

Aggressive positions

In a battle between an aggressor and a defender, the aggressor is likely to move around the recumbent cat keeping its body at an angle to it (above). In part this is to appear larger, but it will also be judging the moment when it can leap onto the other cat. In such a scrap between some household cats, the gaps between clinches are longer than in full fights – lasting perhaps 15 seconds or so, rather than being almost subliminal. During the gaps the aggressor will swish its tail, while the defender on the ground may try a few more front paw bats if it thinks the other cat is coming too close. The aggressor may seem inhibited at times, sitting or giving itself an anxiety lick. However, it is likely to push home its advantage and walk forward towards the other cat's head, with

aggressor will need to get up to re-attack. This gives the defender time to reposition, again spinning around on its back to have its head nearest the aggressor, with its back paws ready to kick it off: the defending cat is now completely the wrong way round for the aggressor.

This upside down position, facing the other cat, looks vulnerable, but is the cat's strongest defensive position (below). A couple of deft defensive parries like this are usually enough to halt the proceedings. The aggressor will lose interest, the defender will settle down, and calm will return to the household, even if the status quo is a little uneven at first.

its own head at an angle, aligning itself ready to leap on.

In the face of this, the defending cat, with ears flat, will normally try more front paw bats and may spin its body to disadvantage the attacker (top), which will try for a head-to-head alignment and a chest grip with its front paws. By turning, the defender can temporarily remove the threat of the aggressor raking with its back legs. It will hold its back legs ready to kick off the aggressor (above). As it leaps on, the aggressor will need to bring its head

in close to the defending cat, simultaneously aiming for a chest hug. As it does so, it flicks its ears back from aggressor threat into flat protection positioning against its head.

If the defender can now spin on its back, it can position the aggressor so that its back feet land on the ground, not on the defender's stomach, and its head and shoulders will also hit the ground. This whole wrong-footing move can be achieved in less than a second, and the

79

Cats usually operate a system of tolerance rather than aggression, and disputes are normally mild and quickly resolved. However, where two large, intact toms behaving territorially are equally matched, and both are flagging aggression with their ears and posture, beware – the fighting that may follow will be extreme (see also pp.78–9).

CAT BEHAVIOUR

Rules of engagement

The menacing sound of tom cats squaring up for a fight is unmistakable. The cats stand with full masculine heads dangerously close, almost touching. One or the other will swallow and lick his lips. Having stood their ground for several minutes, one tom suddenly leaps to bite the other's neck. The attacked cat rolls back to adopt the back-on-the-floor position (see p.78), and each will roll over, trying to obtain a good grasp around the other's

chest. This, plus the intensity of the battle, is what distinguishes the fight between two aggressors from that between an aggressor and a defender.

The cats may crash to the ground and roll over and over, each trying to hold the other tight with clutching front limbs, making any belly raking closer and tighter. The intensity of the kicks can be such that one cat is thrown clear over the other's head as in a judo move – but the thrown cat will leap back and be grappling again within a second. This speed of return is in marked contrast to the more inhibited scrap of normally harmonious cats from

the same household. In a serious fight, the cats may suddenly break, but will stand face to face and re-threaten, then leap again.

When one cat stays down defensively it has moved into the role of defender, and at some point the remaining aggressor will recognize this and cease attacking. Cats do not have a true submission pose, so a defender does not become symbolically subservient and this move from mutual aggressor to defender is the nearest a cat will come to acknowledging that an aggressor has asserted his dominance.

related areas... **43** **44** **46** **47** **50**

52 Dogs and cats

Although dogs will chase cats, they are more respectful of them than may at first seem. Cats have few submissive gestures to call upon. Their comparatively solitary lifestyle means that they have not developed the appeasement behaviours of dogs. This means that when cornered, they can be dangerous as they will defend themselves.

Cat bravery

It is this fight-to-the-last attitude, plus an impressive armoury of fighting weapons, that will make even the largest dog which has cornered a fleeing cat suddenly stop and retreat. It might seem unlikely but cats have the upper hand in many dog-cat scuffles. If, for example, a dog chases a cat up a tree, the cat is secure and merely waits for the dog to go before coming down. If the same dog startles the same cat up onto a garden fence where there is no additional height for the cat to climb, the cat will feel cornered. Consequently, if the dog puts its head up or leaps up, it receives a faceful of claws as the cat strikes at it. Exit dog, fast.

It is such situations that lead to the near legendary tales of 'cat bravery' on behalf of their owners, although the frequency of such stories is far lower than with dogs. One involves a women opening her front door to find a stranger swinging a cleaver down at her head. Her cat saved her life by jumping onto his face from the stairs and scratching him. This apparently gallant act was probably due to the cat being startled, feeling trapped and cornered, and seeking an escape by clambering up!

related areas...  3 10 43 48 49 50

53 Cat talk – meow, trill, chirp

As a small cat, whose main ancestor is the African wildcat, the domestic cat's vocal range excludes the roaring of the big cats, but of the range of sounds it can make, the attention-seeking 'meow' is most commonly heard. This is often at its loudest when the cat comes back into the house and announces its arrival.

A low-key murmur – a quieter and shorter form of the trill – is described as an acknowledgement sound. It is met when you gently put a hand on a near-dozing cat and it gives a small sound response, in which you can almost hear a question mark.

Open-mouth sounds

The sounds coming from a mouth that opens and then gradually closes comprise the range of 'meows', with a fixed vowel-pattern sequence. However, the emphasis, pace and delivery changes the quality of the sounds. These are thought to be 'meows' of demand, begging demand, bewilderment and complaint.

The various 'meows' develop from the kitten's restricted and intense vowel-pattern 'mew'. Whenever even the youngest kitten is out of the nest it will start up its repeat call of distress, to which its mother will respond by coming to its aid. Pick up and hold a week-old kitten for a second longer than it wants to be held and it will let loose a stream of insistent 'mews'! The full meow is not voiced properly in a kitten under eleven weeks. Defensive and aggressive sounds, such as the defensive hiss (below), are made with the mouth held open.

Closed-mouth sounds

Closed-mouth sounds include the most evocatively feline sound, the purr. They also include the rising trill of greeting, where your cat may meet you arching its back slightly, lifting its tail and sometimes lifting briefly on its front paws. The gentle trill of the mother cat responding to her young kittens with a 'come close' sound is similarly structured. Most of the male's chirping sounds during mating, when the queen is presenting in lordosis, are made with a closed mouth. The latter two sounds show similar characteristics; they are both requests to 'come close and make contact'. This reinforces the probability that the rising trill made by your cat as it greets you shares a similar meaning.

54 Cat chat

Studies suggest there is a feline vocabulary that can be linked to particular meanings. Phonetic patterns have been recognized by researchers and among them are the distinctive mating and fighting patterns, purring and spitting, as well as leaving demand, begging demand and complaint.

Messages

In 1944, Mildred Moelk distinguished 16 utterances in the adult cat, which she found to impart specific meaning. While Desmond Morris has suggested that the vocal sounds of cats can be summarized into just six messages: I am angry; I am frightened; I am in pain; I want attention; come with me; and I am inoffensive. However, there are many shades of meaning depending on how and where these sounds are delivered.

For example, two facing cats, usually males, will caterwaul as part of their sabre-rattling threats. The shrieks, screams and snarls of the active fight are unambiguous. In the violent sounds of aggression and defence the throat is held tensely, producing the harsher sounds of growling, snarling, hissing and spitting. The shrieking response to sudden pain also falls into this category, which is not the same as the deep distress howl. The sexual calls of the queen on heat and her mating cry seem to have a combination of a strained intensity and vowel sound.

Roaring

The distinguishing vocal feature between the small cats and the big cats is that small cats scream while big cats roar. This was been believed to be due to the hyoid cartilage being bony in small cats and flexibly cartilaginous in the big cats. This theory has recently been challenged by the discovery that the big cats have a large pad of elastic tissue connected to the upper part of the vocal cords. This allows the roar and is missing in the small cats.

Talking to people

As they grow into adults, house cats 'find their voice' and through interplay with their owners they can modify remarkably the sounds they make. It is not only that we encourage our cats to 'chat', but that they actually note our use of vocalization and 'turn up the volume'! Women are generally more interactive vocally with cats and consequently cats respond more. Cats returning from outdoor forays are more vocal and demonstrative in greeting than are confined cats. Once physical contact is made by rubbing, vocalization normally stops. Some cats, as they come into the home, call ahead in a slow regular way, particularly the vocally loud Siamese.

related areas...   30   31   51   53   55

The title of Paul Gallico's much-loved book *The Silent Meow* is based on sound observation, for there are a number of cats that go through much of their lives virtually mute. They will look up plaintively at their owners and silently mouth a 'meow', but this will not affect their ability to communicate.

CAT BEHAVIOUR

Non vocalization

In such cats it is not that they are mute physically, but that they give only the behavioural appearance of meowing, without the vocalization. This can also be seen in cats that are very vocal normally, but will on occasion just mouth the meow. This is an inhibited form of what has been called the begging demand, which itself is an inhibited form of the 'demand' sound. Owners can cause their cat to repeat the demand sound time after time by looking at the cat and mimicking the noise. However, there needs to be a motivation for the cat, and this is usually provided by distance. For example, if a cat sitting outside by the door looks up and sees you at an upstairs window, it will make the inhibited demand. If you then repeat either the sounded or the silent meow, depending on what the cat is making, it will continue with its inhibited demand.

Finding a voice

My old female cat, 'Mr Jeremy Fisher', who reached 25 years of age, was a silent cat. For many years she would otherwise interact completely normally, except that when she opened her mouth to meow no sound came out. She was used to travelling in the car on occasional long journeys. However, one day I rashly drove through the centre of London, and looking out through the window at the traffic chaos she suddenly found her voice – and never lost it again! From that day on she used it as if she always had. Among breed cats the Russian Blue is considered by many breeders and judges to be the 'most silent' and when it does vocalize, to have a 'quiet voice'. This is consistent with the perception that Russian Blues are withdrawn and shy, and inhibited with vocalization.

Purring

A mother cat with a line of suckling, purring kittens seems the ultimate scene of contentment. Cats also purr for themselves: when they are comfortable, when they greet a cat companion, or when rubbing and rolling. Purring can occur in juveniles eliciting responses from adults, and adults reassuring juveniles. Queens purr during mating.

Why purr?

Although the cat uses the purr in a range of close-contact encouragement and reassurance situations, it is probable that it originates as a co-operative sound between kittens and mother during suckling. Kittens suckle for prolonged periods, and the purr can be made while on the teat with a closed mouth. Purring by their mother and littermates calms kittens and keeps them together in the nest. Purring provides kittens with a contact call which keeps them together while the mother is away hunting, and it is so quiet that it is not overheard by other predators. The purr is needed as the female rears young unaided in the cats' social system.

As well as the reassurance and contact conveyed by purring, there is also a statement of existence: 'I am here, I am here'. This is what you hear when you sit on the bed and up comes a purr from an unseen cat under the duvet, or when a vet examines a cat.

Virtually all mammals suckle and very few purr. However, the whole cat family and their nearest relatives, which include civets, genets, mongooses and hyenas (although they look like dogs, they are closer to cats), will purr in one way or another when mothers suckle young. Tigers, in the wild and in captivity, produce single-stroke, purr-like sounds from deep in their throats on exhalation. Although it is anatomically different, the cheetah produces a true purr, like the small cats. The big cats have a more flexible hyoid cartilage and cartilage pads in an area of the throat that is more flexible than in the small cats. This allows them to make a resonant roar but may prevent the double-stroke purr.

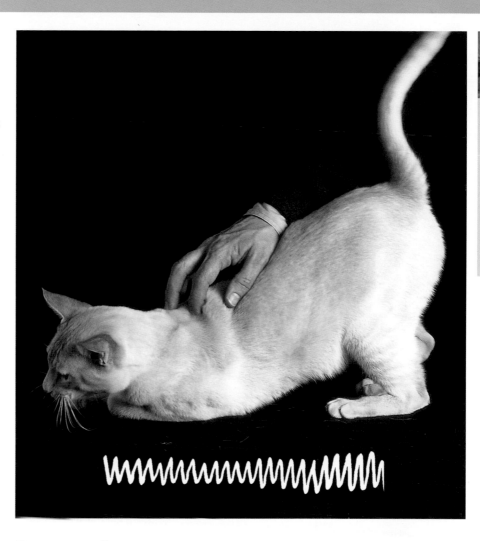

Purring facts

The average domestic cat purrs with a fundamental frequency of 26.3Hz (cycles per second) (ranging 23–31Hz), and this does not change throughout the adult life. Purring is louder when the cat holds its mouth open, but typically it is only 84dB just 3cm (1½in) in front of the mouth. It is lower and quieter than most sounds made by the cat.

related areas...   **34**   **53**   **54**   **55**   **57**

Paddling and purring

When your cat leaps up onto your lap, before settling down for a comfortable snooze it is quite likely to paddle on your chest or knees with a slow, rhythmic open and closing of its front paws, and this will often be accompanied by purring. This behaviour can be surprising or even amusing to someone who hasn't experienced it before.

CAT BEHAVIOUR

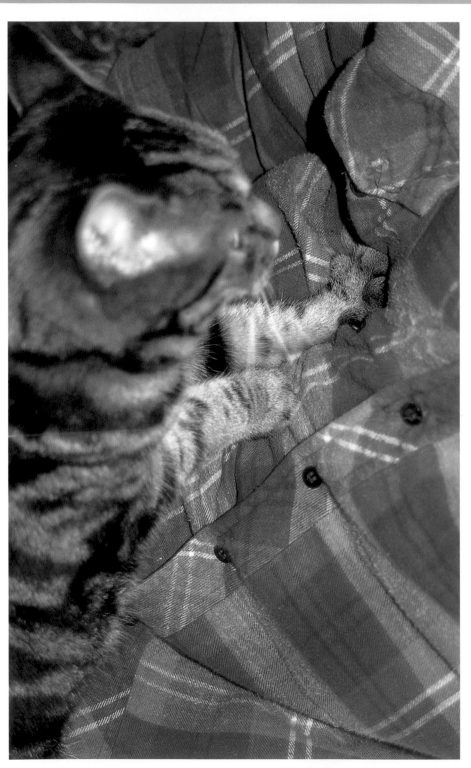

A reminder of kittenhood?

From the age of three weeks until weaning, kittens spend a lot of their time paddling and purring around their mother's teats. The movement of their paws simulates milk flow. Our warm laps and large size seem to bring out this kittenish behaviour in our cats.

However, it is not so cut and dried, for adult queens coming into heat carry out the same opening and closing of their paws while both paddling and purring. To test if a queen is approaching oestrus, breeders may stroke or pat her along her back towards the tail – if she is, she will elevate her rump and adopt the lordosis position. If you do the same to the cat paddling on your lap you will elicit a similar response. During pro-oestrus the queen will be very friendly and will rub around with her head or neck. Consequently, cats' behaviour towards us can be viewed as part juvenile and part sexual, but clearly affectionate.

related areas...   30   31   34   49   56   96

58 Eye-to-eye

Cats have large expressive eyes and they use them to good effect in their relationships with other cats and other animals. Two major forms of communication with the eyes are conveyed through blinking and staring. These are the reverse of each other, having opposite meanings.

Blinking

A slow blink is very powerful as a reassurance signal and is commonly used between cats when they are sitting or lying in a hunched-up, sphinx-like position. I have used the blink to relax house cats, feral cats and even tigers in the wild. Cats are masters of stealth and to try to creep directly towards them is likely to unnerve them. Instead, it is important to put them at their ease by allowing them to read the signals that tell them you are not a threat. It is vital not to give the impression of approaching, and to perform blinks that are slow and definite, with eyes hooded.

Staring

One thing that filming cats has taught me is how threatening and unsettling they find a continuous stare. It is certainly something that cats use themselves to achieve just that effect. When an aggressive cat is intimidating another with slit-pupil eyes and threatening ears, it does it with an unblinking stare. Cats do look directly at each other at times, such as in the build-up to renewed mating, but then the nature of the eyes is not threatening.

Cats maintaining territorial distance also make effective use of the stare threat. This is commonly seen in the cats in our gardens, particularly in high-density urban areas. They will sit for hours on end, sphinx-like with front paws tucked under, and just stare from a vantage point within their territory at another cat within the territorial limits. It is most commonly seen between queens of adjacent territories, and these 'stare-pairs' repeat the procedure day after day. In our interactions with cats, it is important to remember how intimidating and threatening a stare can be – diffuse your attention when socializing with cats.

related areas... 4 43 44 47 50 52

Domesticating the cat

The main ancestor of the domestic cat is considered to be the African wildcat of North Africa (*Felis silvestris lybica*), which overlapped the Marsh cat (*Felis chaus*) in its range in Egypt along the Nile. Although domestication of the cat may also have occurred elsewhere, the only significant evidence comes from ancient Egypt, where cats were kept confined in temples.

the sun's first rays. The Pharaohs Cheops and Chephren, who built these pyramids, also built the earliest part of the temple of the cat goddess Bastet at Bubastis in the Nile delta around 4,500 years ago.

Herodotus, who visited Bastet's temple in the fifth century BC, recorded that it was the chief annual assembly site for a god. Over 700,000 people made the pilgrimage. At that time the cat goddess was the key female fertility deity, on an equal footing with the Greek Artemis or the Roman Diana. Millions of cats were mummified and buried in Bubastis and at other cat cult centres. Herodotus tells us that the festival dedicated to the cat was celebrated 'with abundant sacrifices' and X-rays have shown that a number of cats had their necks broken. Yet when a cat died naturally, householders shaved off their own eyebrows in remorse, and carried their cat to Bubastis for embalming and burial.

A recent pet

When your cat looks at you it can convey the essence of contentment and trust, yet a second glance can reflect a little of that wildness which mirrors the rest of the family. For its size its range of weapons are as formidable as those of the tiger. As hunters, the cat family is unsurpassed. Our pet cats have retained many features of their wild ancestry. This makes them the most truly enigmatic of animals. The cat retains an independence that is treasured by all true cat lovers.

It is intriguing that the two animals that most closely share our lives as pets

Cats as gods

I believe I was the first to identify the Marsh (or Jungle) cat in one of the earliest cat paintings in Egypt in Khnumhotep's tomb, close to the temple of Pakhet, the cat goddess of middle Egypt. I also found bones of the Marsh cat in the temple, suggesting that it had been kept with the African wildcat (opposite, below). Although the main ancestor of the domestic cat was the

African wildcat, some hybridisation may have contributed to early domestication.

The domestic cat was a species born into this world with the status of a god. This was not just recognition of the 'other-worldly' character of the small cat, but because of its identification with its larger cousins. In ancient Egypt a link existed between the sun's heat and the power of the lion. The lion-bodied sphinx guards the pyramids at Giza, facing due east to meet

today, the cat and dog, are both carnivores and hunters. Yet while the dog was one of the first domesticated animals, the cat was one of the last. This was not by chance but a consequence of their differing lifestyles, and our lifestyle at the time. As herd hunters our activities overlapped those of the wolf packs, and their ability to scavenge allowed them to haunt mankind's camps. The rest is history!

However, it took lifestyle and landscape changes over thousands of years to domesticate the cat. The development of agriculture and subsequent settlement and urbanization, produced the waste that provided scavengeable material in sufficient abundance to support a population of normally lone-hunting cats. When we see feral cats scavenging to survive, we

are watching a replay of the events that drew the cat into our lives. The move by the cat into domestic living has been a survival ploy that has worked spectacularly. While originally the cat had only a local distribution in the Middle East, it is now found worldwide in huge numbers.

Both cat and dog have had a working relationship with us for most of their history. The status that most household cats hold as pets today is very recent. We are still adjusting to that changed role. Its significance should not be underestimated, for numbers and distribution of all other cat species are in decline due to habitat destruction and conflict with man. It has been during the period that the domestic cat moved into predominantly pet status, that the decline of wild cats has been so dramatic. From the mid-nineteenth century

mankind's own numbers and destruction of huge areas of the planet's surface have exploded. As man thrived, so did the domestic cat due to the massive increase in food supply for house and feral animals.

59 Why we keep cats

For much of mankind's 3,500-year relationship with it, the cat has been used mainly for its rodent controlling skills. Only with the advent of cat showing in London in 1871, did it become acceptable as a pet to a wide spectrum of the population. Its spectacular rise to become probably the most popular pet in the world is therefore quite remarkable.

Companionship

When we hold our cats and confide our innermost secrets to what is often our closest companion, this intimate act is being repeated all around the world. Yet just a few generations ago such universal devotion to cats would have been unthinkable. Our social changes to accommodate the cat have been dramatic, but no less than the huge leap taken by the solitary hunting cat to become a pet.

In essence, we behave in our relationships to cats as if they are people, and cats behave in many ways to us as if we are cats. Both cats and dogs are mammals of sufficient size and response to be companionable, but their relationship with us is quite different. Due to their wolf ancestry, dogs have a hierarchical social structure. They are secure with the owner

as the dominant partner and what we regard as affection from the dog is largely appeasement behaviour. Cats are not very hierarchical in their social structure and have no need of appeasement behaviour, therefore our relationship with them is on a more equal footing. However, there is a blurring of roles in our relationship with cats, for sometimes they behave towards us as adult cats, sometimes as if they are juveniles, and sometimes as if we are sexual partners!

On your street

As you walk around the streets of Britain you will find a cat at virtually every other house, sitting in the doorway sunning itself. There has been a massive increase in cat ownership in North America and

across Europe in recent years. In Britain in the early 1980s there were around 5 million owned cats but by 1993 this figure had risen to 7.1 million, pushing the dog out of the number 1 slot. In the USA, this happened earlier, in 1987, when the cat reached 56.2 million. This 30 percent increase is largely due to changes in our lifestyles. Professional couples who are both working find the regular tie of taking a dog for a walk too restricting. Dogs are less convenient for urban living. Young couples who are delaying having children are keeping cats instead. However, because they go out to work many people have a second cat so that the two can 'keep each other company'.

In the UK, owned cats peaked in 2000, at nearly 8 million, and there were 7.7 million in 2002, by which time the number of dogs had declined to 6.1 million. In the USA, owned cats numbered 77 million and dogs 61 million. In the USA, 36 percent of homes had dogs and 33 percent had cats (2003) while in the UK both were 19 percent (2001).

related areas...　　42　60　61

Why cats like us

Although cats living in feral groups do interact affectionately and members of multi-cat households may greet each other with head rubbing, and they may lie together, such interludes are often tempered with the odd spat. In contrast, affectionate interactions occur extensively between domestic cats and the people with whom they live.

KEEPING CATS

We are mother

Why should this happen so much more between cats and people than between cats and cats, when we are different species?

Paul Leyhausen suggests that we are similar enough to evoke the cat's juvenile behaviour, but not similar enough to provoke defence and/or attack behaviour. We certainly are the focus for juvenile features of behaviour, from purring to play. This is partly due to our huge size relative to an adult cat, which is similar to the proportion of an adult cat to a young kitten. By sitting on our lap our cat receives as much contact and warmth as it would have from its mother. Our stroking hands are comparable to its mother's tongue, reminding the cat of its mother washing it. Picking up cats and carrying them around, a task previously only done by the cats' mother, reinforces our role as does placing ourselves in the position of the hunter, the provider of food.

Early conditioning

Cats that are not at ease with people do not prolong or seek contact. For example, some feral cats may habituate to someone who feeds them, while others remain distant. It is also interesting to note that feral cat groups are more accepting of members of their own group than outsiders – to our household cats we are members of a common group.

Early conditioning of kittens to people allows them to accept people in a more relaxed way. In addition, domestication has resulted in selection for more juvenile behaviour in cats, not just for them to be more tractable, but also to be more trusting of people.

Friendly communication

When cats meet they often investigate each other briefly, nose towards nose. This may be followed by a head rub, then walking in contact with the other cat's side. However, with strange cats the response is much more likely to be cautious. When we greet a cat they focus on and rub against our hands, having first sniffed a finger. Our hands do not have ears to convey messages and we fairly quickly make the positive move of stroking the cat. It is likely that our success at socializing with cats is due partly to our inability to 'flag' aggressive intentions with ear movements. We both initiate and sustain prolonged affectionate moves, and this is sufficient to foster commitment to us in our cats.

related areas... 37 40 41 50 67 77 79

61 Moggies versus breeds

If you want a cat of dependable character with good health and few behavioural problems, you are statistically better off choosing a moggie. Breed or pedigree cats make up only around 7 percent of the cat population in Britain, Europe and America, yet they form the basis of about half the problem cats seen by animal behaviour practitioners.

KEEPING CATS

Mediterranean, and south and south-east Asia, the warm climate has kept the equivalent to the moggie closer to its Egyptian origins in build. Due to the fear of witchcraft, the cats of Britain and Europe were not tampered with for the last few hundred years, and in consequence have an identifiable shape.

Owner or cat?

The seemingly high incidence of problems among breed cats may be because they have a narrower genetic base, and really do have more behavioural problems. Breed owners also appear to seek help more readily than moggie owners. In addition, the majority of problems seem to arise from keeping cats captive or at too high a density, and this occurs more with breed cats than with moggies.

What is a moggie?

The moggie is the house cat, the pet, the street cat, the farm cat. Moggies are the everyday house cats of Britain, the ancestors of the British Shorthair show cat, and have equivalents in America, Europe, Asia, Australia and New Zealand. In most of these places, the cats have a common solid build. However, in the

Character

Ask any cat owner and they will say that their cat has its own definite character. This applies to moggies but also to the various breeds, although members of particular breeds may share some traits (see opposite). Anyone who has had many cats over the years will remember them all as having distinct characters, and will recall stories that demonstrate a particular aspect of their old friends. Yet behaviourists rarely use words like character or friend, although they do use human terms to describe more negative features, such as aggression. Whether we call it style, personality or character, owners know such features can be identified in cats. Among my own cats, I often used to say of Leroy, the tom, that he was 'laid back', 'Mr Cool', but a 'demon hunter'. In contrast, Tabitha, the female, was 'more nervy'. My previous house cat, Mr Jeremy Fisher, who lived until she was almost 25 years old, was always 'a lady'. For me, such terms encapsulate the essence of my individual cat's behaviour.

related areas... 37 59 60 62 63

62 Breed characters

Early conditioning and habituation to people during kittenhood make a big difference to how cats relate to us as adults, so there must be some caution when generalizing about patterns of breed behaviour. However, comparing specific show bench breeds illustrates some stereotypic breed behaviour. For more breed information see pp.96–9.

Persian or Siamese?

The biggest differences in temperament and behaviour are between the key historic breed groupings. For example, the fuller-figured and heavy-coated Persian is more lethargic than the extrovert short-haired cats of south-east Asia, such as the Siamese. However, the traditional form of the Siamese (bottom) is nothing like as extreme in its liveliness as the modern, thinner variety. Similarly, the modern exaggeration of the Persian form, with its flatter face and fuller coat, has led to a cat that simply cannot be very active.

The main reason for these broad behavioural differences, along with variation in appearance and build, is that the cats existed separately for centuries, so each of these major groups is genetically distinct. The cat in south-east Asia probably originated from a few individuals brought by sea traders from the Mediterranean. The predominance of the kinky tail gene throughout the region supports this idea. In contrast, the Persian is of comparatively recent origin; ancient Turkish Angora and Angora-like cats from the eastern Mediterranean to the Caspian Sea were crossed in eighteenth-century France and then nineteenth-century Britain to produce the long-haired amalgam.

Further observations

A survey of American show judges and another of British veterinarians identified distinctive breed behaviours and confirmed popular opinion. Generally, Siamese, Burmese and Oriental Shorthairs are seen as the most active, outgoing, excitable, playful, demanding, vocal and destructive breeds. The Siamese's attention-seeking is noticeable due to its vocal nature; it is often described as 'talking'. Persians are seen as reserved and not demanding or giving of affection. Although they will sit placidly for ages, their abundant fur makes them uncomfortably hot on our warm laps.

Himalayans (Colourpoint Longhairs) have an intermediate behaviour pattern between Persians and Siamese, which is more consistent with their ancestry than their primary build. However, their full coats make them just as unhappy about being lap cats as Persians. Behaviour differences are not only due to fur length, though, for the character of the British/ European/American Shorthair is not like that of the Siamese/Burmese group. Similarly, the robust Northern Longhairs, such as Maine Coon and Norwegian Forest Cat and the lithe, playful real Turkish Van cat and Angora are more energetic than the Persian, which is related to their build.

An introduction to cat breeds

What is a breed? The simplest view is that it is a type of cat recognized by a registered body. However, from the biological perspective, criteria for some modern breeds are trivial. In contrast, historic breeds have formed as a result of geographic and therefore genetic separation, so although their development was aided by humanity, natural selection has largely been involved. These ancient types of cat are the most authentic of breeds and were formed long before the advent of the cat fancy.

British, European and American Shorthairs

The British Shorthair should really be the robust moggie (see pp.94–5), but during World War II, breeding was drastically reduced. Then when pedigree numbers were low in Britain, they were bred – for no good reason – to foreign body shorthairs, and then mated to Persians to correct the build. The result was a different cat. It is an attractive animal, but it does not represent its historic lineage, not least because its beak is inherited from the Persian. The loss of the basic mog from British showing would have saddened Harrison Weir (organizer of the first cat show, at Crystal Palace in July 1871) who said: 'a high-class, short-haired cat is one of the most perfect animals ever created'.

The same thing happened in America, but the result was called the Exotic Shorthair; the name American Shorthair was retained for what purports to be the all-American mog (in the early days of the American cat fancy, British cats were mated with American cats).

The European Shorthair has the traditional shorthair build, yet there could be distinctions in breed lines. The 'blue' cats illustrate the differences between 'history' and reality. Tradition holds that Carthusian monks bred a distinct blue cat called the Chartreux. However, to keep the Chartreux in existence, it was mated with British Blues and Persians, which eroded any distinctiveness; it is now usually judged on the same standard as the British Blues. In the early 1980s in Scandinavia a group of breeders began the reinstitution of the selected mog as a showcat, which led to the recognition of the European Shorthair by the Fédération Internationale Feline (FiFe). House cats have been shown in the novice class for European Shorthair at Cat Association of Britain shows as the association is a member of FiFe.

Oriental and foreign shorthairs

The cats of East Asia are distinct from those of European ancestry. Among street cats in East Asia one of the most noticeable genetic modifications is the kinky tail, which occurs in two out of three cats. Its abundance suggests that Arab and Indian seafarers introduced a few cats, one of which had a malformation in the tail, to the Malay Peninsula many centuries ago, and that their genes are still strong in many cats there today. (The extreme form of kinky tail, a rabbit-like bobtail, is the basis of the Japanese Bobtail.) These introduced cats might also have been of slender build, a feature retained in South Asian cat breeds. In Thailand (Siam) centuries ago, the *Cat Book Poems* were written down under royal instruction; these document the Siamese, Korat and Copper and reveal the antiquity of these breeds.

Siamese The Siamese cat was the consort of the monarchs of Siam, and was presented to certain visiting dignitaries in the nineteenth century. At the first cat show in 1871 its remarkable appearance caused a sensation and was a major factor in the show's success. Initially Siamese in the West were only imported in the dark sealpoint, but gradually the hidden inheritance of recessive and colour dilution genes gave the blue, chocolate and lilac 'classic' Siamese colours. Among the temple cats of Thailand there are other colourpoints that have arisen by natural crossing. Breeders in the West have extended the Siamese inheritance into longhaired breeds, making it the main coat determinant (after the underlying tabby) in the show-cat world.

Siamese

Burmese Initially, the Burmese was believed to have been a breeder's invention, as it appeared when a US Navy psychiatrist took home a brown cat, called Wong Mau, from Rangoon in 1930. Wong

Mau showed some point darkening. He was crossed with a Siamese, and the kittens were crossed back to him. In the litter, along with Siamese offspring, were brown cats and a rich dark chocolate cat, designated Burmese. However, brown cats have a long history. They were termed Thong Daeng or Coppers in the *Cat Book Poems*. I found both Coppers and full Burmese feral in Thailand. Western breeders of the Tonkinese (the remade Copper) were delighted to learn that the breed could still be found today.

Unfortunately, fashion has moved the Burmese towards a slighter build in Britain, while the original form has been retained in the USA.

Burmese

Abyssinian This is a tabby although most people do not think of it as one, mainly because it lacks stripes. However, even in the breed form, there are tabby markings on the forehead, face and tail. Breeders have worked hard to reduce these markings; street versions have far clearer face and forehead patterning.

The show Abyssinian's beautiful cinnamon agouti (flecked) coat has the same natural shadowing of the Marsh

Abyssinian

(Jungle) cat. It makes Abyssinian kittens perhaps the prettiest of all. Devotees suggest that this breed has been around since the time of the ancient Egyptians. It is arguable that some of the Egyptian statues show agouti-marked cats, but these could well be Marsh cats, which were kept captive on temple sites.

Korat and Russian Blue The blue cat from the Korat province of East Thailand is one of the true gems of the cat world. Originally a farmers' cat, it is a gentle but lively cat, popular with Thai breeders today.

Although shown in Britain at the end of the nineteenth century, the Korat was ignored because the Russian Blue was already established. The Russian Blue's arrival was attributed to sailors bringing it from Archangel. Even when the Korat became established 40 years ago in America, and was then re-introduced to Britain, there was again resistance due to similarities to the Russian Blue. A post-World War II outcrossing of Russian Blues with Siamese blue points to produce a more foreign type added to the confusion. However, during the 1960s Russian Blue breeders made an effort to regain the original conformation, and the Korat eventually won acceptance.

Korat

Russian Blue

Singapura Only recently recognized as a breed, having been introduced into the USA from Singapore in the 1970s, the Singapura became known as 'the drain cat' because it was said to be so small that it could seek refuge (in the dry non-monsoon seasons!) in the island's drainpipes. It had the distinction of being in the *Guinness Book of Records* as the smallest cat breed in the world, with adult queens weighing only around 1.8kg (4lb), and the toms a couple of pounds more. It was bred initially from just four cats, so care has been taken to avoid narrowing the genetic base too much.

In appearance, Singapuras are agouti-marked, with upper foreleg banding similar to non-breed Abyssinians, but of smaller size. They are gentle and calm cats that move with a quiet manner, but can be playful and have a wide-eyed openness.

Singapura

Bengal A cross made during the late 1970s between a wild Asiatic leopard cat (*Felis bengalensis*) and a domestic cat has resulted in the Bengal, recognized as a new breed in 1983. Its stunning spotted coat, in which it has inherited some of the looks of its wild parent, has led to a rapid surge of popularity and there are already over 9,000 worldwide.

It seems that virtually all species of small wildcat can hybridize with domestic cats. There have been many attempts, but most have produced spitfires! The Bengal cat has – or seems to have – more tractable behaviour. Its 'personality', consistently notable in eight generations, is one of pronounced investigative curiosity, restless liveliness and a dedication to hunting and chasing. The voice, not frequently used, is harsh.

To establish the hybrid strain as a breed, only stable, friendly offspring were selected. The first generation hybrids were not good pets, but the behaviour changed with progressive hybrid crosses. Intriguingly, the early hybrids often preferred to eliminate in running water, a behaviour attributed to the wild Leopard cat. Bengals still have a particular fascination with running water, which is more marked than in fully domestic cats.

Bengal

Longhairs

Original Persian My earliest recollection of a cat is from my childhood days and is of my grandparents' lovely old brown tabby Persian. It spent much of its time asleep in the afternoon sun on the wooden lid of a massive waterbutt at the back of their house. It was a wonderful cat of a type popular 50 years ago with a fine, straight unmessed-about nose and an old style coat that did not need brushing (see p.95).

Angora From Istanbul to Tehran, longhair cats can be found with a slim, warm-climate build. The genetic mutation selection for these longhairs has been favoured by conditions that can inflict severe winters yet scorching summers. The Anatolian Angoras and Vans have an elegant long-faced appearance.

Weir recalled that around 1850 most people referred to longhair cats as 'French cats, as they were mostly imported from Paris'. These were the Angoras, which had travelled to France from the Ottoman Empire to become the darlings of the seventeenth-century French court. By

1903, Frances Simpson, an influential show judge, could find 'hardly any difference between Angoras and Persians'. This was due to indiscriminate breeding between all longhairs, regardless of origin. Fortunately, attention to historic and geographic integrity of breeds has again become recognized as important. The true Angora reappeared in showing in the 1950s.

Angora

Modern Persian The Persians of the type of my childhood companion shared something of their ancestors' build. However, breeding in Britain and Europe shortened the animal's nose to produce what its devotees view as a more appealing face, though its detractors would call it pugnacious. Lovers of the modern Persian longhairs are not concerned by the criticism that by imposing a flatter 'baby' face and a fuller coat that needs daily brushing, they are perpetuating a dependent toy.

Modern Persian

Silver Tabby, Smoke and Chinchilla The longhaired cat exists in an array of types but some stunning coats began to be bred at the end of the nineteenth century. The Smoke Persian was granted its own class in 1893 and the Chinchilla followed in 1894. These emerged from breeding Silver Tabbies, and form a series around an inhibitor gene. In the Silver Tabby, the gene suppresses the yellow banding more than it does the dark lines, so the coat is black tabby on white.

The Chinchilla has the most remarkable of marked coats; it is as if the mist from the ghost of a tabby has kissed the tips of the hairs. Its delicate shading is due to the inhibitor gene suppressing colour in the hair, except at the point where the hair first grows. The difference between the Silver Tabby and the Chinchilla is one of degree.

Chinchilla and Silver Tabby

The Smoke is caused in the same way as the Chinchilla, but its tipping is more noticeable and even. In Cameo Longhairs, orange is swapped for black.

Colourpoint Longhair One of the largest groups of current showbench cats is the Colourpoint Longhair, or Himalayan in the USA. These are a blend of East and West, for they inherit points of colour from the Siamese in the body of a modern Persian. Colourpoint Longhairs were first bred in Britain and America some 50 years ago.

To retain the Persian appearance, breeders usually cross Colourpoint Longhairs with Persians rather than with other Colourpoint Longhairs. As the colourpoint gene is recessive, the resultant solid-colour Longhairs are then crossed with Colourpoint Longhairs, which yields both Colourpoint Longhairs and solid-colour Longhairs. In essence, the result is a coat-colour class of Persian, rather than a separate breed.

Colourpoint Longhair

Balinese The Balinese is a long-haired mutation of the Siamese. It has the body of the Siamese with flowing silky hair. It retains the Siamese's outgoing, talkative nature, but shares with the Angora a near tangle-free coat, and retains an elegant long nose. In recent years, the conformation of the Balinese has pursued a svelte form.

Balinese

Birman The Birman shares the Siamese points and the slightly heavier build of the earlier Siamese type. Its white feet are the distinctive feature: there is a belief that they derive from the cats from Lao-Tsun Temple in Burma. Folklore suggests a supernatural origin for the first cat's white feet from contact with its dying companion, the priest Mun-Ha.

Birman

Somali As the Balinese is to the Siamese, so the Somali is to the Abyssinian. Its very striking ticked coat reveals it has 'the soul of the wild'. The Somali probably originated as a mutation, but it has been argued that the recessive longhair gene stems from early outcrossings to longhairs.

Somali

Northern Longhairs

Those who prefer the older, rugged style of longhair are enthusiastic about the growing interest in Northern Longhairs. The Maine Coon cat from New England is very popular in the USA and has experienced a surge in popularity in the Old World. The similar Norwegian Forest Cat is equally robust with a similar homestead background.

Maine Coon Maine Coons are a no-nonsense cat, as they should be with a history of being farm cats in rugged New England. They are easily the largest of breed cats – a really fine tom matures into his full coat and build at about four years old, and can then weigh as much as 11kg (25lb)! They are seen as 'gentle giants', for they have an easy-going nature combined with the confidence granted by their size.

Maine Coon

63 Odd cats

In recent years there has been an unfortunate move to accept novelty or 'designer' cats. By choosing to select some of these animals as breeds – to the disadvantage of the animals – the health and welfare of the cats have been put in jeopardy, and the physical changes have not been without behavioural cost.

KEEPING CATS

Selecting extremes

One way these changes have come about is by gradual selection towards exaggerated extremes, in large part caused by awarding points for extremes at the show bench. This has produced the modern Persian with its fuller flatter face, in veterinary terms maxillo-facial compression, with a predisposition towards respiratory, pharyngeal and eye diseases. The change from the traditional standard-shaped Siamese to the thinner form has produced more restlessly active cats.

Acceptance of mutations

Recent breeding practice has also been more likely to accept radical appearance changes arising from mutations. A number of these are controversial, not least because of their behaviour implications. The Scottish Fold, with its ear deformity, must be outcrossed to avoid horrific cartilage and bone deformations. The Fold's ears are permanently flattened in a defensive look. The American Curl from California similarly has ears permanently distorted back, which may seem to another cat to be signalling aggression. The inability to move its ears deprives the cat of a major means of communication.

The American short-legged mutation called the 'Munchkin' has been selected purely as a novelty. It cannot jump and climb in the normal way, and lacks the lithe balanced movements of other cats.

Its grooming behaviour is also restricted because of its short legs. Normal behaviour is similarly affected in the Sphynx. Its lack of fur affects its ability to control its temperature; consequently, its free access to the outside world in cooler conditions has to be curtailed.

The Manx

The Isle of Man's tailless cat has been in existence for around 200 years. It is a charming creature, but were this mutation to occur today it would be considered unacceptable to breed it on as it is a dominant gene and homozygotes die before birth while among heterozygotes malformation causes a high rate of still births.

related areas... 43 44 61 62

64 Cats and new homes

When you obtain a new cat, or are moving home with your cat, remember that it is a stressful time for the animal. If it is a new cat, you want it to settle in happily as soon as possible so spend some time on preparing for its homecoming. If it is an existing pet, do not just assume that just because you are already friends, it will gladly accept the move.

Settling in

With a new cat or when moving home with an existing cat, use a carrier to transport the cat and when you arrive put it into a room where it will not be disturbed. Provide some food, a litter tray and lots of reassurance. Once the rest of the house is in a more settled state (if you have all moved), begin to allow the cat to investigate. Do not allow it into the outside world for at least a week.

When you do allow your cat out for a brief sortie, it is safer to take it on a harness and lead. Certainly, ensure that you remain near the cat's entrance back into its new home at first so that it becomes familiar with its safe return route. Do not leave the cat outside alone, but stay quietly with it. Gradually lengthen the time outside, and you will be able to gauge when it can be allowed to look after itself by its growing confidence.

Consider your cat

Moving house is a very stressful time for us, partly due to the separation and loss of the familiar place, friends and memories, and partly because of the trauma of the upheaval and the arrival of the unfamiliar. It is the same for our cats. We at least know why the upheaval is taking place, but for the cat it is just perturbing.

Do not forget about your cat until the last moment; instead put it into a quiet room while the rest of the house is being emptied. If the cat has been scared and has run off at your old home, sit and await its return. At the new home, do not take any risks – do not let your cat outside without supervision until you are sure it knows how to get back into the house and is confident with its new surroundings.

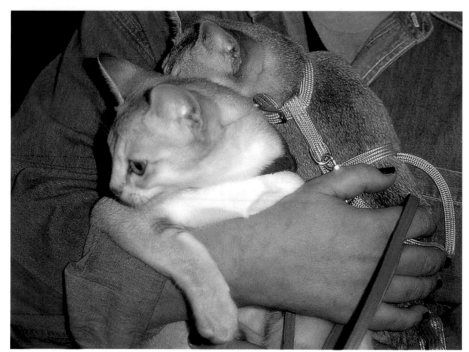

When we feed our cats we are continually being a ready food source. This means that in one sense we play the mother role and reinforce our cats' 'kitten' status. In another sense, as a continuing dependable food source, we are like a rabbit warren or rubbish bins around which cats can structure their ranges.

KEEPING CATS

The need for protein

Cats are obligate carnivores. Don't ever think of making your cat a vegetarian, even if you are; such a diet would kill it. The cat has a uniquely high requirement for protein as it metabolizes both protein and fat, rather than carbohydrate, to produce energy. Cats also need particular amino-acids and fatty acids in their diet. In 'complete' products, manufacturers of cat food provide a well-balanced diet, but this is not always so in the gourmet ranges, so check the label if you intend to feed your cat only on this type of food.

The make-up of canned food is similar to that of prey – around 75 percent water, with dry weight measured components of 35 per cent protein to 10–15 percent fat. Dry foods are used as a convenience, but contain only around 10 percent fluid. As the cat would normally obtain virtually all of its liquid requirements from its food, unless it can compensate by drinking about a third of a pint a day, the urine can become too concentrated, encouraging crystals to form and resulting in kidney damage.

Little and often?

Cats catch small prey, and so repeatedly eat small feeds; if given free access to food bowls, they will eat small amounts 10 to 20 times a day. However, we usually feed them twice a day and they rapidly devour it, which seems to be similar to their attitude to gluts. For example, although my cat Leroy may dispatch a two-month-old rabbit at one sitting, he usually eats half of a three-month-old the evening he catches it and the other half in the early hours of the morning, after a rest.

Eat and sleep

You often hear 'When I come back it will be as a cat for all they do is eat and sleep!' Yet these two features of the cat's life are intricately linked. It is only because it eats the high protein hunter's diet that a cat can invest in such a lot of sleep. This reduces stress and means a cat lives longer than is general for an animal of its size. But the cost to the kidneys of a high-protein diet is a continual barrage of toxic breakdown products. Kidney failure is a major cause of cat death.

66 Hair care

The cat is the most fastidious of animals. Feral cats and many shorthaired house cats go through their lives without anyone grooming them, and they nearly always look immaculate because they do the job so well themselves. However, many of the longhaired breeds require careful grooming everyday.

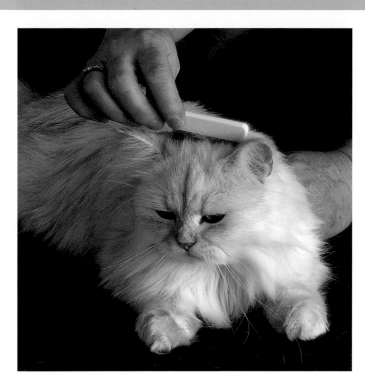

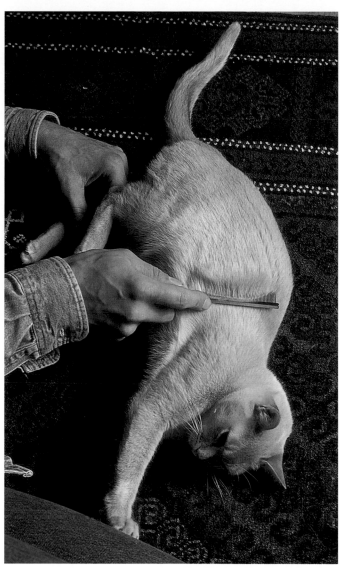

When to groom

This does not mean you should not comb a shorthaired cat, but once or twice a week will be quite sufficient. It will enable you to check for fleas and to remove shed hair, so your furniture is less likely to end up looking like a yak. Combing will also mean your cat ingests less hair and so will avoid hair-blocked bowels.

Longhaired cats fall into three groups: the heavy-coated Northern Longhairs, including the Maine Coon and the Norwegian Forest Cat; the lighter-coated Angoras, Balinese and Somalis; and the modern Persians. The natural coats of the first two groups do not need the intense attention required by the modern Persian. Breeding has modified its coat to such an extent that it is essential to brush and comb it daily otherwise it will become seriously knotted. A cat in this state is a distressing sight, for the animal is unable even to walk properly as its skin is held taut by the knots. This type of cat does not survive in a feral state.

Accustom Persians and other longhairs to gentle grooming from kittenhood so that they do not become agitated; fortunately most Persians have a good temperament and enjoy the attention. Ease out knots by using a wide-toothed comb or by hand. If the coat has become heavily knotted seek a vet's help. In addition,

the buckled tear ducts of flatter-faced longhairs cannot drain properly, so fluid wells out of their eyes and matts the fur. Gently wipe with cotton wool, but avoid contact with the eyes.

The older-style longhair cats do not have the problems of the modern Persians. For example, the traditional Angora undergoes a dramatic moult each spring, for its original home of Anatolia is freezing in winter and blisteringly hot in summer. However, the coat of any longhaired cat can become matted around the anus, and may then become infested with blowfly maggots in hot weather. Avoid this through grooming.

related areas...   **28**   **37**   **62**

67 Communicating with your cat

In many ways I behave towards my cats as if they are human – and I'm not alone in that! Similarly, to my cats I am some sort of cat. We are all a bit confused on the overlap between people and pets. The vast majority of us talk to our cats and they learn how to interpret our words and actions, and in return form their home range in close relation to us.

Family and friends

A survey by Peter Borchelt and Victoria Voith of nearly 900 cat owners visiting four American veterinary hospitals found that 96 percent of household cats were talked to at least once a day. Around 65 percent recognized that they talked to their cats entirely as if they were human, mostly a child. An unassailable 99 percent considered their cats as members of their family. Among those who talked to their cats, only 13 percent said they did so as if they were just pets.

Conditioned communication

In any household there is a mutually understandable cat and human pidgin language that has arisen from a joint need to communicate. Most of us speak to cats as if to children, and at feeding times we may talk to them as if they were a baby, slightly higher pitched, with sing-song rhythms. We tap the plate and use exactly the same wording and intonation each time: 'Do you want something to eat?', 'Here Kitty, Kitty, Kitty'.

Other daily patterns such as sitting down after meals, when the cat may leap onto your lap and settle down for a nap, are sequences that cats recognize and interpret. They also learn to anticipate regular activities like returning from work: being there for the owner's arrival shows an accurate gauging of time plus an interpretation of, say, our car engine noise.

Your territory

When you look at how your cat forms its range, it becomes clear that it relates to you as if you are a cat. Cats don't regard a fence as a limit, but they do look to see where and how we use space. If you never go into your garden, your cat may well have no particular attachment to it. If you love to sit in the garden, you will surely have a feline companion. While a fence may not demonstrate ownership to the cat, it recognizes your presence as declaring ownership and gains confidence in its right to be there because you are there.

related areas... 17 37 59 60 74 78 79

68 Catflaps

For a cat to have its own door to a building is not a modern idea: I used to live in an ancient watermill that had had a cat hole in its door for hundreds of years for the working cats to come and go as they pleased. It was at a height that cats could get through, but too high for rats to reach.

Choosing a catflap

Today's catflaps are an excellent development, for the flap keeps out cold draughts as well. Unfortunately, the simple variety can allow neighbouring cats access if they know how to use flaps and are determined to enter. Although the scent of your own cat on the flap is usually enough to inhibit entry, if you are troubled by other cats, there are the additional options of magnetic release or electronic catflaps. Both allow access only to those cats with a magnet or colour-coded collar tag. Alternatively, many catflaps have a variety of opening settings, so that your cat can come in, but not go out again, or vice versa.

The best catflaps open both ways and are transparent. This makes their use very easy for the cat: it can check that entry or exit is safe before pushing the flap open with its nose or front paws and then step or jump through. Some flaps open only one way and are not transparent, so the cat has to learn to flip up the flap and work its way under it.

Training for the catflap

Initially, fasten the catflap wide open either with tape or a clothes' peg. With a magnetic or electronic flap, tape down or switch off the triggered locking device.

Allow your cat to familiarize itself by sniffing the opened catflap. Encouraging the cat to pop through a few times by calling it is usually sufficient.

Over a number of days, gradually lower the flap until there is only about a 7cm (3in) gap and the cat has to push the flap to get through. Once the cat is coping with that, drop the flap completely, and the cat usually manages to open it.

related areas... 14 15 64 67

Using a collar and lead

If your cat is an indoor and outdoor cat, it will need to have some form of identification. The simplest is the cat collar with a small name tag with your cat's name, your surname, address and phone number. If your cat gets injured or strays, it is vital that you can be contacted. A name tag also identifies the cat as yours, and not a stray.

KEEPING CATS

Fitting a collar

A collar must have an elasticated part so that if it is snagged, the cat can pull itself free. There should be just room for two fingers under the collar; if it is fitted too slackly, snagging on tree branches becomes more likely. In built-up areas a reflective collar makes it more easily seen when crossing roads. A very few cats manage to make a habit of catching a tooth on their collar, and for them the injectable identity microchip is an option.

Cat leads and harnesses

There will be times in all house cats' lives where the use of a lead and harness is invaluable. It is especially useful when you have moved home and are introducing your cat to the outside world after it has become familiar with the new house.

It is vital to allow your cat to become used to the harness indoors. Many cats initially attempt to wriggle or squirm out of a harness, or just flump straight down onto the ground. Let it wear the harness without the lead for a while at first. Lengthen the time it wears it, then connect the lead but allow it to remain slack and preferably do not hold it at the beginning.

Eventually the cat should be reasonably happy to follow you on the lead. If you drop the lead accidentally when you are with the cat in an unknown or potentially dangerous place, do not shout or charge after the cat for this usually encourages it to run from you. It is far better to walk quietly and gently alongside it without looking as if you are about to pounce, and pick up the lead without a fuss when you see the opportunity.

70 Travelling cats

For too many cats, the only journeys they make are to the vets or a cattery, which gives negative reinforcing. At some point in its life you will probably have to take your cat to your vet, possibly in an injured or seriously ill condition when it is important not to add unnecessary stress because you have not habituated your cat to travel.

KEEPING CATS

Learning to travel

Cats can become stressed very easily when travelling by car, and may call out repeatedly. They may work themselves into a state and be sick in only a few miles. In hot weather, it is particularly bad for cats to become stressed in cars. To avoid these problems, it is vital to gently condition your cat to travel, preferably from a young age.

First make sure your cat is happy to use a carrier or it will probably struggle as you approach with it in your hand, especially if you only use it when you visit the vet. Ideally the carrier should be a ventilated plastic one, which gives the cat a feeling of security, and of not being exposed on all sides. Wicker carriers are not necessarily very secure, nor are they easy to clean. Put in

some newspaper, which cats love to sit on, and gently put your pet in but don't shut the door. Leave the carrier around the house for some days so that the cat can use it as a nest should it care to. From time to time, walk the cat around the house in the carrier.

Next, put the cat in its carrier into the car, and sit with it there. Repeat this for a few days, then again with the engine idling. Introduce the cat to very short journeys and progressively longer ones. Ensure that you drive smoothly and not too fast, for the first few miles of the journey. Motorways are generally easier for the cat as they have fewer bends, roundabouts and junctions. Eventually and with a little time and patience your cat should be reasonably happy about car travel.

related areas...   60   64   67

71 Keeping more than one cat

Plenty of people have more than one cat and they get along just fine, but it is not always straightforward introducing a new cat into an established household. This is because cats are basically solitary animals and need time to adjust and accept a newcomer. There may be a certain amount of scrapping at first as familiarization takes place.

gradually familiarize themselves with each other's scent. When eventually they do meet there will be sparring, but it should be less disastrous than it could have been.

Aggression

No matter how well cats are integrated low-speed inhibited fights may break out around meal times, or seasonally with winter 'trapped-in' blues. When an aggressor approaches an upright cat, the defensive cat may crouch and flatten its ears to minimize the target, but raise a wary paw and even strike the air with a mixture of hissing and growling. However, this is not a submissive pose, for the cat is ready to retaliate.

If one cat runs in fast to attack a standing cat without warning (which can happen with displaced aggression, as when a specific 'target' is missed but the steamed-up cat runs on to another, or in some territorial attacks), then the attacked cat rears up with the momentum and bats back. Both cats will rear up, but the defender will use alternate front paw swipes, standing tall in the same position it would adopt when lying on its back during a full-blown scrap.

Kittens

The easiest way to have more than one cat is to begin with two kittens, as they will come to behave as if they were littermates, even if not from the same litter. Cats who live together from kittenhood tend to retain a grooming bond and they will groom each other from time to time (allogrooming). This will also happen with non-related household cats.

New cats

When introducing a new cat into a home with a resident adult cat, make it possible for the resident cat to 'meet' just the scent of the new cat for a while to establish the right of the newcomer to be present. To do this keep the newcomer in one room initially; when the resident cat is absent, allow it into other rooms then put it back in its own room. In this way the two cats

related areas... **17** **18** **19** **28** **40** **64** **93**

72 A good age

Cats wear age with great dignity. Even when very elderly, they still enjoy life, particularly if it involves snoozing in the sun. My own old female cat, 'Mr Jeremy Fisher' (below right), reached almost 25 years of age. She remained remarkably fit, and until just a few months before her death, still walked along the top of the garden fence.

Life expectancy

Intact toms can expect to live at least two years less than neutered toms. Neutering queens has little effect on their longevity. Around 12 to 14 years is a good age for a neutered cat, male or female; few will live above 16. Some, like Jeremy, will make it into their twenties.

Special care

As the cat becomes less active, you may need to trim its claws more frequently. Its walking may become stiffer and coat less lustrous. Pay particular attention to the cat's teeth and gums. If it does not stress the cat, it can be helpful to clean its teeth to prevent build up of tartar and gums inflammation (gingivitis). Your vet can remove the tartar to prevent tooth loss. Giving the cat some real meat to chew on occasionally can help clean its teeth.

The most usual cause of weight loss in the elderly cat is partial kidney failure, often caused by its high protein diet. You may notice your cat drinking more. Some cats respond to treatment and a modification of diet, which will provide a reasonable quality of life for a while, although long-term prospects are not good.

Euthanasia

Your pet is a loved member of your family and may well be your closest companion, so your grief will be real if it has to be 'put to sleep'. Your vet will appreciate your dilemma and advise you accordingly. But it is your pet, and the final decision will be yours. Many vets will put your cat to sleep at home, should you wish; this normally involves an injection of barbiturate. You will also need to discuss with your vet whether you wish your cat to be buried in your garden, or buried or cremated at a pet cemetery, rather than being disposed of in a more routine way.

Around 3 percent of all veterinary consultations involve euthanasia. These can be upsetting for the vet as well, despite being routine. Courses in bereavement counselling are becoming normal practice in veterinary schools.

73 Neutering and vaccinating

Unless you intend to breed or show your cat, you should consider having it neutered. It will avoid most of the fighting, the pungent spraying of the tom and his roaming, the queen's demanding calling when in season, and any unwanted kittens. Regular vaccination is essential to avoid unpleasant and unnecessary disease.

KEEPING CATS

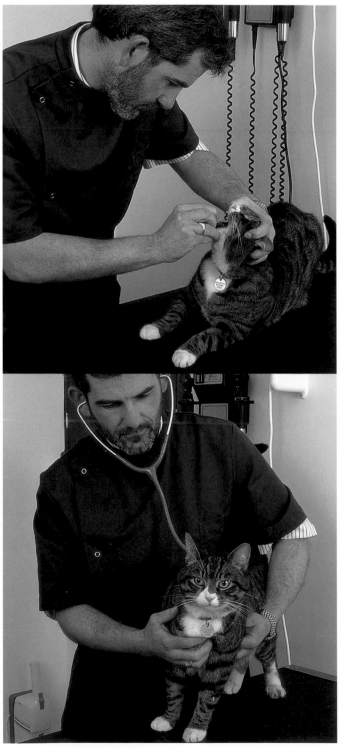

Age and stage

In the female the neutering operation is termed spaying, and most vets prefer to undertake it at five months. In the male it is termed castration, and most vets suggest this occurs at around six months.

Spaying involves an operation to remove the ovaries and much of the uterus. It is a routine procedure for vets and is performed under a general anaesthetic, so the cat knows little about it. As with all operations, she will need to be starved of food for about 12 hours beforehand. When she returns home, which may be after an overnight stay at the vet's, give her easily digestible food for a day or two. You may need to have her stitches removed in a week or so. Castration is also carried out under general anaesthetic with the same preparatory starving period. Because it is not such an invasive surgery, the cat can come home the same day and will need simple food and rest. There are normally no stitches.

An ancient practice

Most people assume that the control of the cat's sex life by neutering is recent. While this is true for the female, castration of males is an ancient practice. It has long been used on horses, bulls, boars, rams, cocks and cats to make the animals more manageable and for food animals to lay down more fat, and may have been carried out since the beginnings of husbandry. In the early seventeenth century Edward Topsell noted accurately that in domestic cats: 'The males live longer if they be gelt or libbed'.

Vaccinating

Two vaccinations are currently routinely given to cats against Feline Infectious Enteritis (FIE) and 'Cat Flu' respiratory disease (Feline Viral Rhinotracheitis (FVR) and Feline Calicivirus Disease (FCD)). Once the passive immunity received by kittens from their mother's milk fades, it is important that they are treated. Your vet will advise you on timing. For show cats and any cats spending time in a cattery, it is essential that they receive their injections. In those countries where rabies exists, it is advisable for your cat to have inoculations against it.

related areas...　　　29　31　32　35

74

The indoor cat

Unfortunately for American cats, the USA is leading the world in making cats confined and dependent. Twenty-five years ago most cats in the USA, like Britain and elsewhere today, were indoor-outdoor cats, but a creeping fear of the outside world as unsuitable for pets has gripped America. The main hazards for cats are seen to be traffic death and disease risk.

Weigh up the risks

Before keeping a cat confined you need to weigh up the possibility of disease risk and road death with the probability of confinement behavioural problems. Understandably where traffic is dense there is a reason to be cautious: in Baltimore, for example, it was found that a cat had a one in ten chance of being killed in a year on the streets. However, fears about traffic deaths are usually exaggerated. In addition, in the USA, disease risk figures are often expressed as if preventative vaccinations did not exist. Rabies is endemic in the USA, but the main risk of the disease is from dogs; cats rarely communicate rabies.

As a result of increased cat confinement – 55 million are kept indoors all the time – countries such as the USA have seen an increase in behavioural problems. Urinating around the house, 'clawing the drapes' and aggression are now significant parts of the American cat's lifestyle. Despite this, at a meeting of cat welfare organizations, one senior executive was heard to say, 'Now I assume one thing we can all agree about is that all cats should be kept in all the time?'. Ironically, the old natural breed of which America is rightly proud, the Maine Coon, developed as a robust cat purely because of its outdoor barn life.

Declawing

Declawing is often justified as the last ditch stand against 'aggressive' or furniture-damaging cats, but it can be the first resort, carried out by vets on kittens. This barbaric, unnecessary operation has become common in some countries. Declawing is basically mutilation and should be considered as such by welfare groups. The British Veterinary Association and the Royal College of Veterinary Surgeons are firmly against declawing, and consequently it is not allowed in Britain. Behavioural approaches are far better, and today practising cat behaviourists are often available for consultation via veterinary referral.

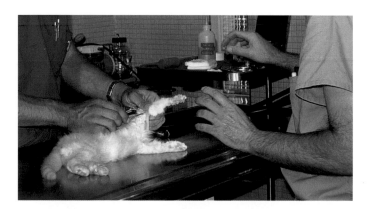

related areas... **84** **87** **89** **90** **98**

The attraction of catnip

If you are trying to grow catnip (*Nepeta*), you will know about its powerful attraction for some cats. The volatile oil in the leaves and stems stimulates the olfactory bulbs at the front of the cerebral cortex, which then produces altered states in the cat. The domestic cat is not alone in its fondness for catnip, even lions respond in a similar way.

Varied response

Not all cats are affected by catnip. The reaction seems to be inherited as a dominant gene by about 50 percent of cats, and does not show until sexual maturity; post-weaned kittens around 9 to 12 weeks old begin to show interest. There may be a breed linkage too, as Siamese seem less affected.

The most common response is to sniff, then to lick the plant. Some cats, particularly older ones, will drool noticeably. Quite often, these reactions may be followed by a small amount of chinning (see p.33). These animals often then lose interest. However, those showing a keen focused interest will endeavour to pull the herb to their head with their paws while rubbing against it, perhaps even head rolling. With this group, if an attempt is made to pull the catnip away, the cat may strike out with claws outstretched, even with cats that have no history of striking out at people; owners need to be aware of this risk. Such behaviour will abate within seconds of the catnip being removed. Shy cats often have an inhibited response, whereby all they do is sniff the catnip with some interest, and even keen cats will eventually reach a satiation point. Cats may also eat catnip, but when taken internally it actually has a calming effect.

The behaviourial response in both sexes resembles that of the female rolling oestrus and post-copulation response and is done by both neutered and intact animals. From this it seems probable that the smell of catnip resembles the female cat's sexual odour. The desire to roll in catnip may arise from changes in skin sensitivity or glandular secretions that may be caused by oestrogen.

It's in the smell

The wild form of catnip is most attractive to cats, perhaps because cultivated varieties, such as *Nepeta racemosa* or *N.* 'Six Hills Giant', have a much weaker scent. If you wish to grow the stronger-scented wild form for your cats without having it destroyed, the trick is to grow it through other plants, which will protect it.

related areas...   **7   11   12   18   29   30**

76 Sleeping with your cat

Some people wouldn't dream of going to bed without a mound of cats all over it, while other owners wouldn't contemplate such a pet invasion. A survey by Barrie Sinrod of 10,000 pet-owning households in the USA found that 60 percent of pets sleep in or on their owner's beds.

Do not disturb

The group most likely to cuddle up with their pet is young women between 18 and 34 years old. In contrast, married men over 45 tolerate the pet only if it sleeps on the foot of the bed.

Cats appreciate the prolonged, restful and close contact they can achieve by sleeping with us. Given their small size relative to people it is remarkable that they aren't squashed, but somehow we allow for them, even in our sleep and move carefully so as not to disturb them. Given half a chance most cats will try to burrow under the duvet. Many owners draw the line at this. If prevented from lying directly on its owner, a cat usually prefers to curl up in the hollow at the back of the legs.

What about sex?

The Sinrod study found that 73 percent of American pet owners had sex while their pet was in the room. This demonstrates the privileged role pets play in our lives, for while we don't view our pets as inanimate, and in many ways relate to them as members of our human group, we don't normally allow other family members to be present at such times! It can't be that we think cats are oblivious to what is going on, for they often react empathetically.

Our behaviour towards our cats is often quite blatantly sexual in origin. In Sinrod's survey 81 percent of cat owners were found to kiss their cats – nearly 20 percent more than would kiss their dogs. Due to the softer nature of their fur we stroke cats, while we tend to pat dogs. Our stroking of a cat is reinforced because it is reciprocated. When we repeatedly stroke a cat on its back, it raises its rump and tail and lowers its forelimbs. This is a mixed message: in part the raised tail greeting, but also a sexual statement.

Our own sex will usually have an effect on our relationship with a cat. Perhaps because of the long-standing feline/feminine relationship, which dates from ancient Egypt, many women believe they empathize more naturally with cats. Whatever the basis for that belief, women are more likely to feed cats, go down to their level, and speak gently and more frequently to them. Single women spend more time interacting with cats than those living with partners.

related areas...   24   25   26   29   67   78

77 Stress busting

Cats are good for you! Stroke a cat and your stress levels drop. Among the people who benefit from owning cats are those with stressful professions, such as doctors, and those who live alone, such as the elderly. No matter who you are, interacting with a cat, for example, playing games with it, is fun and serves as a distraction from everyday cares.

KEEPING CATS

Cat cures

For some years research has shown that pet ownership is good for your health, and now the study of 'companion animals' has become respectable. Cats Protection, a leading cat charity, surveyed owners and found that the reduction of stress, and the relief from depression and anxiety were major perceived advantages of living with a cat. Many long-term psychiatric hospitals and old people's homes now have resident cats whose company is enjoyed. Even strays can be welcomed for the role they play in cheering up a captive audience.

Cats Protection discovered that 'eight out of ten caring organizations found that cats helped people get better'. The elderly or AIDS sufferers with pets are less likely to have depression.

Pets help institutionalized or isolated people feel more comfortable, and are a reminder of normal home life. Although dogs are often also useful in this role, too, the cat's silky coat makes it more strokable than the rougher dog's coat, so making the stress reduction more effective. A US study found that men owning cats or dogs had lower heart rates and blood pressure than those without. Pets have been found to enhance the recovery of cardiovascular patients.

related areas...　　59　60　67　76　78　79

Lap cat

There is something very flattering about a cat choosing to jump up onto our lap and settle down for a sleep. And we should be flattered – when cats sit on our laps this is a positive action, as free-living adult cats avoid body contact, even with other cats of the same group for most of the time, unless permission is given.

KEEPING CATS

Comfort zone

In addition to reminding the cat of suckling, and being warm and comfortable, we normally invite a cat to sit on us by putting our hands forward. We then reinforce this invitation with stroking, which the cat sees as a combination of adult rubbing and maternal licking. Nevertheless, cats do not like being fiddled with too much, particularly by strangers, and when selecting whose lap to sit on will often choose someone in the group who is not being too demonstrative – usually the unfortunate cat hater!

Not all cats like sitting on laps. The modern Persian, for example, finds this cosy position a little too warm for its liking and it prefers to be petted while sitting on a chair arm or the floor. Nervous cats may find a lap a little too close for comfort and instead of curling up comfortably may perch on a knee with all front paw claws out like miniature crampons.

related areas...   34   57   59   66   67   77

Despite having left kittenhood behind, many adult cats like to continue to play. This is good for their health, especially if they are mainly kept indoors, as it keeps them fit and allows them to practise all their different hunting moves. If your cat shows signs of wanting to play with you, don't be afraid to join in, it is all part of the fun of owning a cat.

KEEPING CATS

which is a flexible rod with a string and small toy on the end. For kittens around the 'teenage' time of three months old, or the thin-bodied form of Siamese, which doesn't slow down much in adult life, the wand provides the fun of pursuit without perspiration for the owner.

More confident cats will often initiate pouncing entrapment games, where the cat sees and responds to movement alone, such as when something is moved under a piece of material or a rug. Try moving your toes around under the bedcovers to encourage your cat to pounce. A development of this type of game is when your cat tunnels under an overhanging bedspread or discarded jumper, or goes behind a curtain, and follows and captures a pencil or similar object that you run across the otherside of the cloth.

Adult house cats will often play by themselves, suddenly having a mad chase after their own tails interspersed with exaggerated licks, or wild dashes around the house, or play hunting by batting around a piece of paper. This behaviour is often retained from kittenhood.

Cat gyms

The advent of the cat gym has been a real boon for many cat-owning households. Gyms provide scratching posts, and most importantly somewhere to clamber up and from which to sit and watch the world. They need to be carefully sited, however, and you need to spend some time playing with your cat on them, otherwise they will simply gather dust. One of their greatest values is that they provide a place for play and communication, recognized by both owner and cat.

Favourite games

Grabbing and holding games are popular. Staircases are great places for this sort of game. When the cat is on the stairs, move a pencil or something similar past the bannisters on the other side, so that it passes in and out of sight. Once you have her interest, the cat will carry out a number of the moves she normally uses in the capture and recapture of small mammals. Although her main move will

be to thrust a paw forward and grab the pencil, she will also anticipate, select and change the gap through which she thrusts this paw. As the cat is employing a hunting grab, she will be using her claws for the strike, so take care when you play this one! The cat will also try to grip the pencil and bring it to her mouth to chew.

Most cats also enjoy pursuit games – anticipating, pouncing and running after a length of string with or without a toy at the end, or the modern version of a 'cat wand',

80 Cat school

Training a dog is 'relatively' easy, but training a cat is much more of a challenge and the techniques used are totally different. This is because a cat does not fit into a hierarchical social structure as a dog does. The simple dominance techniques used in dog training are therefore inappropriate for cats.

Your place in a cat's world

When a cat hunts it does so alone, so co-operation via aggression as found in dogs does not occur, and therefore ordered instructions will have less significance to a cat. When cats do come together and form a group the interactions can be categorized as more affectionate than aggressive. Although it is possible to establish relative hierarchies among a group of cats, it is less significant and of a lower key than in the dog world. So, for example, once you have trained your dog to carry out a command, it will continue to follow your instructions. But you can tell a cat to 'get down off that table' and to an extent it may do as you wish while you are around, but not necessarily when you have gone!

Active and passive deterrents

Passive deterrents work better in modifying your cat's behaviour than active ones. You can fall back on active deterrents when necessary, but to avoid weakening your bond with your cat it is vital that the cat does not realize that you initiated them.

One of the simplest active deterrents is a ball of paper that you can lob at your cat if it is making mischief, but it must not be seen to come from you. It has the decided disadvantage that your cat may think it a game and chase after it! Alternatively use a water pistol; again, it is vital that you are not seen to aim it at your cat. As a technique it should not be overused.

A method employed by animal behaviourists uses an upside-down mousetrap. For example, a cat that repeatedly digs up a large pot-plant can be dissuaded by this method. The trap mechanism is set and placed carefully upside down on the pot soil and covered slightly with a piece of paper and soil. When the cat starts to disturb the soil, the trap makes a noise. I am very wary of this method, for cats' paw bones are small and easily damaged.

Passive techniques are usually easier, both on your cat's and on your nerves, and do not jeopardize your relationship. For example, the inverted mousetrap for large house plants can be replaced by putting a handful of mothballs in a pierced bag on the soil. Cats dislike the smell – but so might your visitors!

related areas... 87 91

Hybrid vigour

Moggies, 'average Joe' cats, are good, gutsy animals that have a fantastic pedigree going back unhindered through the mists of time. Because of their near random mating they have enjoyed the best possible breeding programme for countless generations. Their survival and subsequent breeding derived from natural selection, favouring characteristics that were important and necessary for life. This is an unbeatable combination for healthy animals, producing a natural perfection of design and function.

Moggies are best

The media runs an unwitting 'conspiracy' against the poor old moggie because of the desire to see variety in photographs, among other things. But far more people live with moggies than breed cats – 90 percent of UK and 60 percent of US house cats are moggies. And it is not only picture editors that like to see variety. The high-profile events that promote cats – namely the major cat shows – primarily feature breeds and breeding, rather than moggies and selection of good pets. Of course, breed cats can and do make good pets, but as millions of people will testify, so do moggies.

Why I like moggies

I admit to a bias because my cats are moggies. I choose to have moggies as I believe they are proper cats – the essence of cat – and not genetically messed about. Among cat writers this must put me into a fairly serious minority, for traditionally

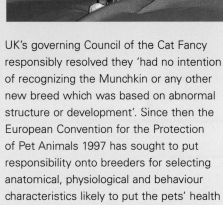

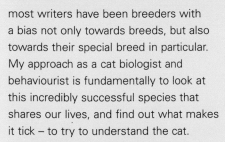

most writers have been breeders with a bias not only towards breeds, but also towards their special breed in particular. My approach as a cat biologist and behaviourist is fundamentally to look at this incredibly successful species that shares our lives, and find out what makes it tick – to try to understand the cat.

Moggies on average live much longer and more healthily than breed cats as they are genetically more robust. Over recent years breed cats seem to be reaching better ages than before, but usually with significant veterinary attention. In addition, in the real world, the majority of cats are moggies, with pure breed cats a minority. Areas of geographical isolation have historic breeds as street and house cats unconnected to the cat fancy world. In some countries the local moggie population is made up of the original cats of what has become a cat fancy breed, such as the Angora in Anatolia, the Siamese and Korat in Thailand and the Japanese Bobtail in Japan. It took the

occupying Americans after World War II to point out to the Japanese that the Bobtail was special; in the same way, it is easy for us to underrate the real British, European and American Shorthair on the streets, for to us it is just 'the moggie'.

Cat mental and physical health

Inevitably, breeding for showing narrows genetic diversity for any line. Competing against written standards has pushed breeding to extremes, where Persian faces became flatter bringing breathing difficulties and choosing disadvantaged mutations, such as the Sphynx, became more acceptable. It cannot be right to choose to breed to disadvantage an animal's health for the sake of novelty.

Bringing these issues into the public arena with my BBC TV series *Cats*, I was heartened that, in response, the

UK's governing Council of the Cat Fancy responsibly resolved they 'had no intention of recognizing the Munchkin or any other new breed which was based on abnormal structure or development'. Since then the European Convention for the Protection of Pet Animals 1997 has sought to put responsibility onto breeders for selecting anatomical, physiological and behaviour characteristics likely to put the pets' health and welfare at risk.

As we are not the same species, it is remarkable that cats and people can and do live together with so few difficulties. After all, there are enough problems when people live with people! However, since the 1980s there has been a massive increase in reported cat 'problems', or antisocial behaviour. Three factors came into play at the same time as this noted increase in problems. The first was the advent of cat behavioural practitioners, who not only give advice, helping owners to do something about their cat problems, but have been able to record the problems more rigorously than was done before. Secondly, across North America, Britain and Europe there has been a huge increase in multi-cat households. Thirdly, and most significantly, there has been a trend – spreading first across North America and then elsewhere – of confining cats inside houses or apartments.

121

81 Fleas

Grooming will soon tell you if your cat has fleas, if its scratching or sudden attacks of washing have not already alerted you. Comb your cat on some white paper, and if characteristic black specks appear, you have found flea droppings. If your cat has fleas, so does your house, and both will need treating.

CAT TROUBLES

Coping with fleas

Fleas are host specific, but if for some reason a cat is away for some weeks, they will have a desperate attempt at feeding on us, which means being bitten. The fleas lay their eggs on carpets, bedding or crevices in the floor, as readily as on the cat. Warm summers and central heating boost their numbers.

A vacuum cleaner will normally contain the flea problem around the house, augmented with an anti-flea house spray. The most effective way to kill fleas that are living on the cat and to prevent re-infestation is to use a liquid insecticide, which is absorbed into the body and kills fleas when they bite the cat. It is obtainable at your local vet practice and your cat will need to be known by them before they can sell it to you. The correct dose is contained in a flat pipette and you simply drop it out onto the back of the cat's neck. Such treatments generally last up to a month. Oral dosing of the cat to control the fleas is also popular. Other possibilities include flea collars, which are helpful, but should not be used on kittens. Examine the neck area a few days after introducing your cat to a flea collar, as the skin of some cats has an inflammatory reaction to them. In warm parts of the USA, such as California, an electronic collar is used to deter fleas from living on cats. Insecticidal sprays and powders are effective, but many cats find the hissing from a spray unnerving, so a pump action may be better. Sprays and powders only kill the fleas on the cat at the time. As flea eggs hatch the cat will need retreating.

Cats can develop tapeworms from catching prey, but the most common tapeworm, *Dipylidium caninum,* can also be caught by a cat swallowing a flea during grooming. Although the immediate host is normally a rodent, this parasite's eggs can be eaten by the flea larvae and then taken up by the cat. In addition, some cats develop a flea allergy and the animal's repeated washing of the affected area worsens the situation. This may need veterinary attention.

related areas... **82 83 85**

Ticks and other external parasites

Cats are generally very clean animals and suffer few unpleasant parasites or external ailments. Fleas are their most common pest and they are quickly and easily recognized and dealt with (see opposite) but you should be aware of the others so that you can treat them if necessary.

Ticks

About 80 percent of ticks found on an afflicted cat are around the ears. Vets often recommend the application of alcohol or insecticide before removing the tick. Use tweezers to remove it cleanly, taking great care to pull vertically so that the mouth parts are not left in the skin, otherwise these will form an abscess.

Ear mites

These minute animals are the most common cause of problems in the cat's external ear, and will spread to other cats and dogs. Kittens are particularly vulnerable and a plug of brown wax caused by a large number of mites can form in the ear. Treatment is essential – vets will prescribe eardrops – otherwise a secondary infection can cause further damage to the cat's ear. Unfortunately, regular treatment is detrimental at a time when the young cat needs to develop confidence with its new owner.

Harvest mites (chiggers)

The tiny red dots moving around on the cat's legs, feet, head and ears in the autumn are harvest mites that can cause irritation. Flea treatments usually kill these pests too.

Fur mites ('walking dandruff')

These are normally spotted when the cat appears to have dandruff on its back. Fortunately the mites are not common, as people can become accidental hosts. The mites can be treated with flea preparations.

Lice

Lice are uncommon in healthy cats but they can be found on sickly animals. The eggs ('nits') stick to the fur and look like fine dandruff. They are controlled by flea treatments.

Careful and regular attention to your cat's health should ensure that it stays free of most pests. If you spot something that looks like a problem, don't hesitate to get it assessed by your vet.

CAT TROUBLES

83 Internal parasites

Although it may seem rather unpleasant to us, an active hunting cat will naturally pick up internal parasites from an intermediate host such as a rodent or bird. Luckily, these pests are reasonably easy to treat and the best way to do this is to have a regular worming routine. Your vet will be able to provide advice and treatments.

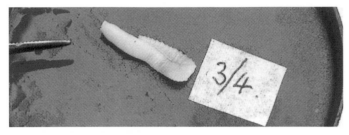

Tapeworm and roundworm

As its name suggests tapeworm is a flat tape-like parasite with ridges along its body. While grooming your cat you may find evidence that it has tapeworm in its intestines from what seem like grains of rice in the coat. More disturbing to most owners is the appearance of a small, flat, white, moving creature in the fur near the cat's rear end. These are motile segments broken from the end of the tapeworm inside the cat.

The hunting cat can also pick up roundworms, which look like wiry white worms with pointed ends. Kittens can be infected during birth. You may find roundworms when your cat brings up a hairball. Obtain treatment for tapeworm and roundworm from your vet; this is usually in the form of a tablet that can be given with food or as a separate dose.

Toxoplasmosis

Toxoplasmas gondii is a single-celled organism that has the cat as its primary host. With the growing tendency to use cat litter, its life cycle needs to be understood because of the potential risk to unborn children.

Cats can be infected with the organism through their prey-catching activities. An infected cat will shed oocysts in its faeces. These can be picked up directly by another cat and infect it, or it can be picked up by any bird or mammal – which includes us. We can also be infected by eating and handling raw or undercooked meat or by not washing our hands after gardening or cleaning out litter trays.

In most people, infection may not cause much effect, but in those with reduced immunity it can be serious. Because unborn babies do not have a fully developed immune system, they are at greatest risk. The effects of toxoplasmosis include stillbirth, mental retardation and blindness.

Cats are fastidious in their cleaning so there is little risk of infection from handling them, but pregnant women should avoid contact with soiled cat litter. Use disposable gloves or, better still, someone else should be responsible for changing the litter. If the litter is changed daily the oocysts will not become infective in that time so the risk is greatly reduced. Other than in warm climates, most people are infected by undercooked meat rather than directly from faeces in soil or litter.

related areas...   28   65   81   82

84 Confinement stress

Confinement and the stress it can induce are major causes of behaviour problems in cats. Even when allowed outside the range of most cats is shrinking. In dense urban housing a female house cat may be limited to a range of 0.02ha (0.05 acre); what is worse – houses in which owners may confine their cats are only a tenth of that size.

A cat's personal space

Keeping additional cats in such a confined space compounds the problem. Furthermore, as cats relate to us as if we are some form of cat, any increase in the human population in that space – including the arrival of a new baby or partner – will aggravate the situation. Plus in small featureless apartments cats can become bored. Owners using confinement as a way of protecting their cat from the outside world of traffic injury and disease, or who fear the cat may not return, have traded these dangers for confinement stress and all the problems this involves. Ironically, the ready availability of cat litter has led to a huge increase in unnecessary confinement.

Confinement also results in a reduction of the cat's range of stimuli, hunting potential and escape options. A stressed queen may respond by abandoning her kittens, engaging in excessive neonatal grooming or suffering reduced milk production. Stress causes physiological changes: the sympathetic autonomic nervous system responds by increasing heart rate, changing blood flow and releasing adrenalin, ready for 'fight' or 'flight' and with the indoor cat commonly leads to such problems as fouling, spraying, aggression, excessive grooming and eating disorders.

Aggression between confined cats

With territorial mammals like cats, an initial aggressive interaction can establish relative positions of dominance. Normally the dispute is settled by one withdrawing from the scene, while the other gains the territorial rights to the area. Where a number of cats are housebound, their territorial limits have been imposed on them. Any aggressive interactions that occur cannot therefore be resolved by the loser withdrawing from the other cat's area, and it will have to endure closer contact with the dominant cat than it would like.

Captivity stress like this can be very damaging and the prolonged biochemical effects may cause a whole range of pathological conditions, from fertility problems to heart failure. When cortisol levels remain high during stress, the allergic and inflammatory responses of the body are reduced, making the animal more vulnerable to infection.

Solutions

Caring owners need to balance the relative risks of their local area carefully before choosing to confine their cats.

Allow confined cats outside. Do this gradually preferably on a leash initially; the cat needs to assure itself of its range and route home.

If cats remain confined then a great stress reducer is to give them the scope to climb up. Provide a cat gym and additional 'retreat shelving' around a room. (You put up shelving for plants and books, so why not your cat?) It also increases the range size. Consider making an extension via a catflap to an external meshed 'conservatory'.

Giving access to a bedroom can reduce stress as the cat will gain comfort from your smell and the sense of contact with you it can obtain there.

related areas... 68 73 78 85 93

85 Excessive grooming

There are a number of causes of overgrooming, but stress is among the most common, with flea infestation also being high on the list. The stresses of confinement in particular can cause a problem with overgrooming. All cats may suffer due to boredom or anxiety, but Siamese and Burmese are particularly prone, as are nervy Abyssinians. Cats will rarely undergroom.

CATTROUBLES

Fleas versus confinement

Signs of overgrooming can be seen on the lower back, abdomen and inner thighs. Loss of hair behind the ears or on part of the back caused by repeated, vigorous scratching with the back feet usually arises from a reaction to skin parasites.

If the cat develops a sudden urgency in grooming, it is always sensible to check for fleas. Comb the cat on white paper – black specks of flea droppings will be seen if the parasites are present. A cat's attack on fleas can lead to skin irritation, which in turn can cause the cat to continue to overgroom to the point of creating near baldness in the affected area. Take note of your cat's behaviour: when flea infestations take hold in part of a building that a cat normally uses, the cat will reduce its time in those areas. At such times, which can coincide with hot weather, the cat may even try to avoid walking on the carpet in infested areas, and will negotiate its way about on the furniture.

Solutions

Where fleas are the problem, the first priority is to remove them. This normally involves the use of a proprietary pesticide sold specifically for the purpose (see p.122). You will need to treat the house at the same time as the cat, as most fleas are hit-and-run merchants and will lurk in your carpets until they are ready to strike again. It may be necessary to repeat the treatment: check the instructions given with the pesticide or ask your vet.

Boredom from confinement can be alleviated by giving your cat more stimulation. This could take the form of providing an 'entertainment centre' based around a cat gym (see p.116).

If the problem is density stress, whether caused by other cats or by people, the exact cause needs to be identified and removed if at all possible.

Overgrooming can also arise when a dependent cat is left on its own for longer periods than previously. In this case, if more time cannot be given to the cat, the closeness of the owner can be mimicked – for example, by leaving around recently worn clothing with the owner's scent on it – to provide reassurance.

86 Eating houseplants

As cats are carnivorous they do not have the teeth to chew and grind vegetation. One look at your cat in the garden as it awkwardly chews off a blade of grass with its side teeth and then gulps it down unmasticated will convince you that it is not a herbivore! Nonetheless, cats do eat some vegetation, mainly grass and leaves.

Provide greenery

Eating plants may provide roughage to aid digestion. When cats vomit up hairballs, grass is usually entwined, and it may assist in removing the discomforting mass. Whatever the reason, if you have confined cats it is sensible to provide a pot of grass in the house, to reduce the likely damage to potted plants. Avoid keeping cats confined with access to any plants that are poisonous to them. A number of houseplants have been connected with the poisoning of cats, including poinsettia, philodendron, ivy, dieffenbachia, azalea, Christmas cherry, and even mistletoe and holly, common among Christmas decorations. When vases of cut flowers such as sweet peas, delphiniums and lupins are added to the list, an owner's anxiety escalates! The danger from house plants is not usually as extreme as from toxins such as antifreeze, but for some cats, particularly confined ones, it can be serious. Usually there is a localized ulceration and irritation in the mouth, sometimes accompanied by gastric disturbance.

Solutions

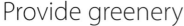

If the cat is caught in the act of eating houseplants it can be dissuaded by a water pistol, or a small beanbag, aimed unseen by the owner. As these active deterrents can misfire, and also require your constant presence, it is probably more effective to try passive techniques.

Position houseplants so that they are less accessible, but beware of cats climbing onto shelves. Placing the plant on a sheet of aluminium foil may not look attractive, but it may be effective in deterring the determined nibbler.

Some cats repeatedly dig around houseplants in large pots, trying to use the compost as litter. Again, blocking their access is effective, but so too is placing mothballs in a muslin bag on the surface of the soil, as cats dislike the smell. It can also prevent them from damaging the leaves. Vinegar and other unpleasant-smelling substances can also be used.

87 Fouling indoors

At least 10 percent of house cats will have a problem with fouling at some point in their lives, with inappropriate urination being twice as likely as defecation, and it is the major problem reported to pet behaviourists. Urine spraying can be a problem with Siamese while Persians are particularly prone to soiling. Don't confuse spraying with urination (see p.130).

Why does it happen?

The most common cause of fouling indoors is owner failure to clean the litter tray. Cats normally bury their faeces, an activity related to territorial confidence. Your cat may not feel safe using the litter tray. In addition, indoor-outdoor male cats may be less at ease with eliminating indoors.

Cats that are allowed outdoors are far less likely to be a problem, for they tend to both urinate and defecate towards the edge of their territory. However, both confidence and the weather can affect this. Frost and snow can restrict digging, although some will cats use snow as if it were soil.

Fouling may be caused by confinement stress (p.125). In this case, you need to deal with the fouling as outlined (see box), and tackle the confinement problems. Even indoor-outdoor cats can become trapped in the house. Timid cats may feel nervous about going outdoors, especially where there is a high cat density, and in multi-cat households, one cat can prevent another from using the catflap. Additional cats or people inside the house can reduce a cat's territorial confidence and lead to soiling.

Diseases like cystitis, which middle-aged female cats may develop, can cause fouling. Easy access to cat litter and antibiotics should soon resolve this. Elderly cats may have mobility problems, which can affect their ability to eliminate in the appropriate place.

Solutions

Site the litter tray where your cat feels safe using it. A tray hood may provide a sense of security. Avoid placing the tray near the cat's food bowl.

In confining the cat you are reducing its choice of latrines; it might like more than one litter tray.

The choice of litter can be critical. Try several types; those that absorb urine and form clumps are generally best.

Clean a fouled area in the home thoroughly so as not to encourage reuse. There are products made specifically for the purpose. Avoid those that may be toxic to cats, such as those containing coal-tar. Having eradicated the smell, change the geography of the site to discourage the cat, perhaps by laying down a sheet of aluminium foil, which some cats don't like walking on, or putting ornaments or furniture in the way.

You may feel irate about fouling, but any punishment or show of aggression will simply increase the cat's anxiety and the likelihood of a recurrence. Instead, analyse why the problem has occurred and try to address the cause.

related areas...   **17**   **48**   **50**   **68**   **84**   **88**

88 Not burying droppings

When there is a territorial dispute between male house cats, both intact and neutered toms will leave droppings prominently sited and not buried. Farm cats that bury faeces around the farm may leave them exposed elsewhere. House cats prefer to bury their faeces on the edges of their range, which often places them in the neighbour's garden!

What might be the problem?

Although it may only be a minor inconvenience to you if your cat doesn't bury its droppings, it could indicate a deeper problem for the cat. Cats are quite sensitive souls, and need to feel confident even to go to the loo. They become concerned if other cats are about, for while using a dug latrine they are vulnerable to intimidation. Consequently you may find that, particularly in the winter, as you come home or go out into the garden you are accompanied, as your presence gives protection.

Lack of sites

Cats usually prefer to leave their droppings semi-peripherally to their confident range, but are restricted by available sites. Lawns and concrete are not enticing, and gardens with weeds and rain-packed soil present few opportunities. In summer, female cats in particular may find hard-baked soil difficult to dig and you could give them a helping hand by turning over an area for them to use once in a while. This might discourage them from using the next-door neighbour's fine tilth. If you find your garden is a communal loo, your best defence is to have a cat of your own and your garden will be dug over less!

How it's done

When cats dig they take their weight on their back legs, and alternating their front paws dig towards themselves, digging deeper as they go. In an average garden soil some 22 paw scoops are usual. When the cat is using its latrine it adopts a characteristic position with its tail up, at up to 50 degrees from the horizontal. Once it has eliminated the cat will then sniff and cover, and repeat until it is happy.

related areas... 17 87

89 Spraying indoors

One of the major problems for most cat owners, sometimes even those who allow their cat freedom outside, is that of spraying, which makes up around 45 percent of complaints about soiling. Yet, unless the cat is an intact tom, such spraying is often not caused by their own cat but by an interloper from nearby.

CATTROUBLES

Why do cats spray?

Intact males use spraying as a form of territory marking. Castration normally reduces its frequency and pungency. Neutered toms that are stressed by the arrival of new toms in their domain may well spray, but it will lack the all-invasive pungency of that of an intact male. Even queens may deposit urine in a male-like way during their breeding period. For an intact tom, the odour of his own spray provides reassurance of his right to be there, and where other scents are detected he is likely to repeat his marking with fresh spraying. Many stud toms will not mate unless their mating pen has been properly scented by spray.

Solutions

Castration generally eliminates the problem of spraying, but one in ten toms will remain a persistent sprayer. For these, treatment with progesterone is normally effective. Interestingly, studies have shown that neutering early does not make spraying any less likely.

Using a water pistol distantly and unseen when the cat is spraying can help to dissuade him. Aggressive irritability by owners is much less helpful.

Try to analyse where and why your cat sprays. There are some surfaces that can almost impel a sprayer to spray. In the outside world, the size, shape and height of most car hub caps encourage spraying. Start looking at your home with this perspective and you will soon realize not only where such sites are, but how few they are. These can then be made less accessible with a change of local geography!

In multi-cat households where spraying is a serious problem, identification of the perpetrator is not always easy. It is possible to 'label' the spray by having a veterinarian inject a suspect cat with a fluorescent marker dye. Over the 24 hours following injection the sprays can be looked at with ultraviolet light – the marked cat's spray will glow bright green.

If it is not one of your own cats that is doing the spraying consider buying a catflap that only allows your cats access to the house, such as one that operates with a special collar.

90 Damaging furniture

A major problem for owners of housebound cats is the damaging of furniture. Even cats allowed access to the outside world will damage furniture, although not as much. Scratching is primarily a marking behaviour, so it is difficult to prevent; your best defence with a scratching cat is to provide something for it to get its claws into.

Sites and deterrents

In the outside world, the most frequently used surface is the bark of a favoured tree, and cats commonly use the front of the arms of armchairs as 'trees'. The cat will tend to use the same spot time after time, for one of the functions of clawing a tree is to leave a visual territorial mark. Consequently, to yell at a cat after you have allowed it to develop a regular scratching post is unlikely to be effective, as the cat is drawn to the visible damage. You need to prevent it early on.

If the cat's favoured scratching post is wooden furniture then you can use passive deterrents in the form of a strong-smelling polish, or vinegar (check first that this will not damage the surface), which the cat will not like. You could place half an orange

alongside the problem spot for the same reason. On padded furniture you can cover the arms with another less attractive material or aluminium kitchen foil.

Then, you need to redirect your cat's action onto a scratching post. A rush mat on the floor will be readily used by some cats but not touched by others. There are specially made, commercially available posts constructed with sisal string, carpet or a similar surface on a wooden post; they are also easy to make. If you have a cat from kittenhood, you should encourage it to use a scratching post. If a cat starts to damage a chair or tableleg then place the post directly in front of the position. When it attempts to claw the furniture, gently transfer your cat across onto the post. Some people find the active deterrent of the water pistol useful when their cat is in the act of clawing the furniture – but remember the cat must not see it being fired.

Declawing is a barbaric, disabling mutilation and should not even be thought of as a means of control for this problem.

91 Dangerous climbing

Cats have an insatiable and perfectly understandable desire to get up onto higher levels. They are, after all, tree-climbing mammals that equate safety with being up high, well out of trouble, in a place from which they can survey the world around them. It is this that drives cats to leap up onto furniture in preference to walking across the floor.

CAT TROUBLES

Why is it a problem?

The kitchen in particular is a dangerous place for the cat that wants to 'get up'. It is essential, of course, that cats do not get onto the hotplates of cooking stoves, and it is far from ideal to have them walking on food preparation surfaces. However, cutting up and dishing out their food on these surfaces does mean that they will be attractive to cats. When a cat leaps up inappropriately many owners just scream 'No!', which is of limited effectiveness, particularly as yelling at your cat can weaken the bond you have developed with it. In addition, although the cat may understand that you do not want it there and will humour you while you are about, it may see no reason for the same restriction when you are not. Usually, adult cats will be more sensible than kittens with heat.

Solutions

Try to alter your home to make danger sites less accessible – for example, by leaving objects on surfaces, which will discourage a cat from jumping up onto them. This becomes increasingly necessary if you have a number of housebound cats, for due to territorial tightness they will be particularly keen to get up onto spots which they feel are secure.

Provide some new surfaces, such as cat gyms, and allowing cats up onto non-damaging surfaces like internal windowsills. Do not worry that providing alternative sites for the cat will confuse it, for the very concept of not climbing is completely alien to a cat.

The limited use of a water pistol, with the water arriving out of the blue and apparently not from you, can be invaluable for deterring cats who appear to be oblivious to danger. The cat then connects that particular spot with the very real danger of a water squirt.

related areas... 2 15 26 79 80 84

92 Rough play

Most of the time play between cats and ourselves is within recognized limits, with both sides being genuinely playful. We tend to be fairly gentle, mindful that the cat is smaller than us and has claws. On their side, cats are aware that we are much larger and more powerful than they are. However, there are times when play can become rough.

Playful becomes rough

When a cat has been playing co-operatively with an owner, it may suddenly grab the wrist with its front paws and vigorously kick with both back legs simultaneously, or alternate individual back legs, and it may even attempt to bite the wrist. This is normal defensive fighting behaviour where a cat on its back rakes the other cat's underside with its back claws. (When using alternate feet even at the inhibited rate on our arm the usual rate of kick at 4 per second is faster than the more measured double kick at 3 per second.) This behaviour understandably causes concern; it is the most likely time that an owner will receive scratches.

What has happened?

The play has heightened the cat's mood, and the grabbing and kicking happens when the cat has rolled onto its back and the owner has attempted to tickle the cat's tummy. This is the area that is vulnerable during a full attack, and it may be that the contact with the stomach or your looming hand triggers the response. We feel the cat is behaving in a 'Jekyll and Hyde' manner, but to the cat it may seem that we have transformed from stroking in the same way as its mother's tongue used to, to suddenly threatening a full adult fight.

There are clearly variations between different cats, and there is a suggestion that there is a tolerance threshold of our behaviour, or trust, based on the kittenhood habituation period, so that habituated kittens are more trusting. I find dependant cats less prone to the behaviour.

Extrication

If your cat starts the sequence, pulling away will cause it to grip and kick harder. Go limp and the cat will stop. Distract it with your other hand, then remove your gripped hand and stand up. If you anticipate the cat's move, just stand up and avoid it.

93 Aggressive behaviour

After fouling, aggression in their pet is the second most common reason why cat owners consult an animal behaviourist. Adult cats of the same household, particularly ones that have been brought up together from a young age, are often playful with each other. However, sometimes these games become more earnest, even if not full-blown fights.

CAT TROUBLES

Types of aggression

Male-to-male fighting, territorial aggression and fear aggression are the most upsetting problems for owners. However, in different situations these classifications can become blurred, and may occur together in a single conflict. Maternal aggression displayed by a mother cat defending her young against another, too inquisitive cat, is entirely appropriate and, due to the context, hardly a problem. Redirected aggression is seen in multi-cat households and in areas where cats live at high density. It is most usually redirected at people during a visit to the vet. The anxious cat is held firmly and treated by the vet, but on its release from the source of danger the cat may lash out at its owner, redirecting its aggression. If this has occurred before, it can be anticipated, and with care avoided.

Threat aggression is one of the key problems associated with multi-cat households. It is usually seen as food is about to be put down. Due to the density of the cats, some will be anxious about obtaining their share and almost invariably the same cat will turn upon another that it can intimidate easily, which again is usually the same cat each time. This type of aggression can be greatly reduced by feeding some of the cats in different areas.

Solutions

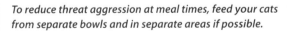

To reduce threat aggression at meal times, feed your cats from separate bowls and in separate areas if possible.

Neutering should significantly reduce male-to-male fighting. Persistent scrappers may benefit from treatment with a female hormone.

Take care when introducing a new cat or kitten to the household. The simplest way is to bring in two kittens together, and they will grow up and behave as if they were littermates. When introducing adult cats, allow their scents to meet before they do. Let one move around in the home in the absence of the other, then reverse the situation. When you eventually allow the cats to meet, anticipate some skirmishes.

94

Armpit rubbing

In our armpits we have scent glands that produce smells which contain some sexual aroma. However clean you are, there will be a residual amount there. It should not surprise us that, with their sensitive noses, cats will notice such things about us – when it has been found that even people can tell the sex of another person by the smell of their sweat alone.

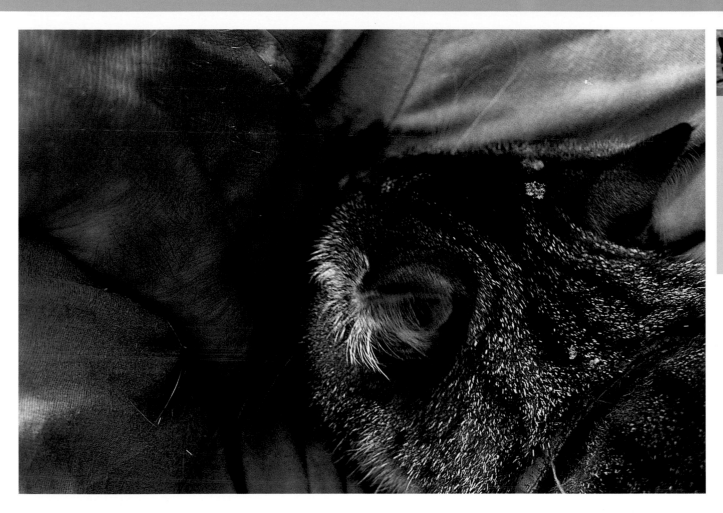

CATTROUBLES

Our attractive aroma

Cats are attracted to our aroma and this may lead to armpit rubbing. This is when your cat starts sniffing, then burrows its chin and head into your armpit, rubbing its nose right up into the area of sweat production. If this is tolerated, the cat will repeatedly burrow and rub; it may drool with its mouth partly open, and may even grip your clothing briefly with its teeth. If your shoulders are uncovered, the cat may similarly tug at your armpit hair and even lick your sweat.

This behaviour is virtually identical with that of a cat sniffing and rubbing on the catnip plant (see p.112). If stroked even lightly during this time, the cat is likely to raise its rump and tail readily in a sexually aroused fashion. If not interrupted by your hysteria, your cat is likely to go on for around a minute and a half before becoming satiated. The similarity of the cat's behaviour with armpits and catnip is due to a common sexual odour in both. It has been suggested that the cat is also seeking the lanolin 'fur' smell.

The attractiveness of the sexual aroma of the axilla and genital areas of worn clothing is probably the reason why cats like to lie, sleep and paddle on their owner's discarded clothes. This is also partly due to the comfort of the soft clothing and the reassurance of the owner's unique smell. The reassurance factor appears to be paramount, as it is dependent cats that are most attracted to warm discarded clothing.

As you are much taller than your cat, you can easily stop this behaviour as it happens, or even prevent it, by simply standing up. However, you may find friends begging you to allow it to continue for its amusement value to them!

95 Eating odd items

If you are wearing a jumper and your cat starts paddling and purring, you may be protected by the texture of the garment. However, the lanolin smell from the wool may induce the cat to drool and suck at it. You may need to curb this habit, particularly in cats that drool so much that the woollen item becomes a wet mess.

CATTROUBLES

Who wool sucks?

There does seem to be a strong genetic predisposition to wool sucking, with some breeds being determined wool suckers/eaters. This is most common in Siamese and Burmese, which can behave quite obsessively in this way. The majority start with wool, and some cats will also eat cotton or synthetic fabrics. In addition other strange objects, such as clastic bands and paper, may become the focus of attention. I once found a feral cat that had eaten a small metal box – whole! The causes for this odd behaviour will not be the same in every case. For example, an adult cat developed the habit of chewing and shredding paper from having been provided with newspaper bedding in its box. It then extended this habit to rather more significant sheets of paper in the house.

Stress and boredom can cause a cat to react by turning to paddling or wool sucking, particularly if it is confined inside its owner's home. Anxious, dependent cats in particular may also develop such behaviour. Although it may seem amusing, it has potential health implications for a serious wool sucker or eater of any other inappropriate materials.

Solutions

🐾 *Act in the same way as a mother cat when she prevents suckling. As the kittens are approaching the time of weaning and she is cutting down on their milk, she will lie over on her nipples or get up and move away to avoid being continually pummelled. You too can move aside or away.*

🐾 *Aim to give more access to the outside, especially for a confined cat.*

🐾 *Try playing more with your cat. More time and reassurance can be a short-term help for an over-dependent cat, and even leaving material around with your odour on it can be of value. But for the over-dependence itself, you should look for a more long-term solution.*

🐾 *Using nasty-tasting substances seems to have only limited value in preventing wool sucking.*

🐾 *Reassess your cat's diet. It is noticeable that regular prey-hunting outdoor cats are less likely to be obsessive eaters of strange materials, and offering your cat interesting and naturally textured food may be helpful.*

related areas... **38** **48** **49** **57** **67** **78** **84**

96 Getting too friendly

Cats can be very affectionate and most of the time we actively encourage and welcome their love and attention. However, there are times when they can become a little too friendly for comfort, and these include when your cat is an over-enthusiastic paddler or an earlobe-sucker.

CATTROUBLES

Painful paddling

When you are sitting down, perhaps watching television, your cat may sit on your lap and start purring and paddling on your chest. Some people worry about this behaviour, but it is quite normal in house cats, for your cat is being 'juvenile' again, reliving its kittenhood and treating you as its mother. When it was very young, foot-paddling either side of its mother's nipple helped to stimulate milk flow. Our larger size and warmth make our adult cats feel like kittens beside their mothers. One drawback of paddling is that the cat's claws will be unsheathed. If you are armoured with stout clothing you may be fine, but if not and the cat's claws are sharp, you may not be feeling as contented as the cat! How often a cat paddles is usually a reflection of its character and how it responds to you. The less confident, dependent cat is far more likely to spend time puncturing your shoulder than the outgoing, laid-back cat.

Earlobe sucking

Some cats develop the habit of sucking their owner's earlobes. This is an interesting variant on wool sucking (see opposite), which is itself an echo of suckling. When earlobe sucking occurs, the person is usually lying down in bed and may even be asleep. Kittens that are weaned too early, or have had a restricted milk supply from their mother, may continue to suck at parts of the bodies of their littermates. They are also likely to be excessive paddlers and over-dependent.

What to do

Neither of these two behaviours is particularly problematic. Standing up or moving away each time are quite effective. One practical answer to painful paddling is to trim the cat's claws to blunt them, while taste aversion can be tried for earlobe sucking. Another obvious solution is not to collude with this behaviour and simply stand up whenever it occurs.

related areas... 34 38 57 77 95

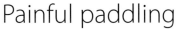

97 Bringing home prey

Even the most ardent cat lover can become concerned when their cat brings home prey. Some owners are upset over the death of a wren, but may be pleased at the dispatching of 10 rodents. In addition, owners often don't like it if the prey escapes inside, and although they may wish the prey had been left alive outside, they want it dead inside!

CATTROUBLES

Cats are hunters

Cats are carnivores and it is not amoral for them to catch food. The reality of keeping a cat is that it will hunt. If you live in a town, you have already reduced your cat's ability to catch much as ranges are smaller. I found the average annual catch of the average London cat to be two items instead of the 14 of a village cat. If you choose a kitten from a litter that was born and reared by a confined mother (so she could not introduce the kittens to prey during the sensitive period approaching weaning), then it is far less likely to develop into a masterful hunter.

You might comfort yourself still further by learning that studies from around the world have found that cats catch relatively few birds compared to small mammals. Furthermore, through our direct feeding of birds, and the provision of good nesting sites in our gardens and buildings, we are also artificially sustaining a much higher bird population than would be found in the harsher environment of the countryside.

Reducing your cat's chances

If your cat is carrying out a capture and release sequence (see p.36), the judicious use of a water pistol can sometimes be effective. The cat must be unaware that it is you doing the firing. The disadvantage of using this technique in the house is that you will probably end up with an escaped mouse hiding behind your furniture. If this happens, then the Tabor Welly Technique can be helpful. As mice and other small mammals tend to run along the edges of rooms, if you position a tall boot on its side along the wall ahead of fleeing prey, with the open end towards the prey, it will gratefully dive into the security of the dark tunnel. You can then quietly take boot and animal outside to release it.

Cats are much more successful at catching birds on the ground than in trees or on bird tables, so feed birds at high levels and make your bird table less cat friendly (see p.40). Time is the key factor, for the longer it takes a cat to get up, the more time the bird will have to spot it and fly off.

98 Fat cats

It was once possible to say that cats rarely have feeding problems – there have always been far greater difficulties with dogs. However, surveys in the USA have revealed that up to one-third of household cats are overweight, mirroring the increase in obesity in the human population. Weight problems are becoming more common in Britain and Europe.

Overfeeding versus confinement

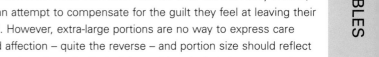

Presenting a cat with over-large portions of food is a major cause of feline obesity. Another contributing factor is the huge increase in confinement of cats, which has been observed in the USA. This results in a dangerous reduction in activity levels due to the restricted area, and an increase in boredom. Owners who go out to work often leave out more food for their cat than they should, in an attempt to compensate for the guilt they feel at leaving their pet. However, extra-large portions are no way to express care and affection – quite the reverse – and portion size should reflect the cat's real needs. Part of the problem is that, in response to market forces, cat-food manufacturers have aimed to produce highly palatable foods, which encourage cats to overeat if given the chance. In addition, the increase in multi-cat households in recent years means that tensions can run high at feeding time, accentuating the tendency of some cats to gorge, while others will eat less than they need.

When weighing your cat, remember a few breeds like the Maine Coon and Rag Doll are large, as are unneutered males (lower picture). Some cats gain weight as they become older and less active, although it seems the most 'at risk' period is around seven years of age.

The convenience of dry food has led to its widespread use, especially in the USA. However, the reduced water content means the food is nutritionally more concentrated, so owners should feed their cats proportionally less. Unfortunately, many still put out the same volume with the result that their cats become obese. It has been found that obese cats over eight years old have a three times greater risk of dying than those of optimal weight.

Solutions

Do not offer your cat portions of food that are larger than it requires to maintain its correct body weight.

If obesity is the result of inactivity caused by confinement, the most effective cure is to give the cat normal access to the outside world once again, allowing it to set its own range. If this is not possible, you should compensate by increasing the time you spend playing with your cat, perhaps using a cat 'gym' to raise the levels of activity.

related areas... 65 66 67 71 79 84

99 Fussy eaters

Cats are notoriously finicky feeders and many households experience a battle of wills over meals, with the owner putting down a particular type of food for the cat and the cat refusing to touch it. Owners will sometimes do this for days before finally giving in to the cat! In reality, cats prefer fresh meat but realistically it cannot always be given.

An iron will

Where food is concerned, the cats' iron will is amply demonstrated by their attachment to particular brands of catfood, which has given pet food manufacturers an advantage over supermarkets trying to introduce their own brands. Cats have reportedly starved to death rather than eat what they find unpalatable. The basis for this stems from the narrow food preference that they learned as kittens: whatever mother brought in when they were kittens they accept, and what they ate then they will have a preference for now.

Undereating

If your cat is usually a good eater but suddenly loses weight and its appetite, consult your vet immediately, as there may be a kidney problem. If you have an elderly cat, keep a close eye on its condition when stroking along the spine, and watch out for weight loss accompanied by drooling, which can indicate gum infection and tooth loss. Other illnesses, especially those that affect the nose, can make a cat go off its food as its initial response to it is through smell.

Solutions

Do not serve a cat its food near a litter tray, which can put it off.

Do not serve food straight from the refrigerator, as cats do not like cold food. It is not just the temperature on the tongue, but the fact that warmer food releases more scent. Cats have evolved to eat food at body temperature (37°C/99°F) and that remains their preference. However, as their interest does not increase markedly between 25°C and 45°C (77°F and 112°F), in all but the most resistant cat there is little to be gained by raising the temperature beyond 25°C (77°F).

Food left out uncovered for too long can age, dry out and even attract flies, and the cat will avoid it.

Cats can sometimes be weaned onto new foods by mixing gradually increasing amounts of the new food with accepted food.

 related areas... 38 65 98

100 Roaming

'Roaming' covers a variety of behaviour patterns: cats that leave home; cats that stay out for a number of nights; cats that have large ranges; and cats that visit other houses. Straying completely commonly occurs when the owners move home and do not keep their cat indoors long enough for it to develop new territorial attachments.

Causes of roaming

Straying can also occur when too many cats are put into one home; then one or more cats will leave to escape the stress. The same situation can cause some male cats suddenly to assume massively larger ranges than they held formely, and similarly greater than the normal size for that area. In contrast, a minority of males patrol a disproportionately large range – up to four times the normal size for the local area – throughout most of their lives; this means that they may be away from home for several nights at a time. I documented the case of a male Siamese and found that his father had displayed similar behaviour, which therefore may have been inherited, genetically or even by being learned. Both cats could also be aggressive towards people, and were assertive in demeanour.

Some cats may have a number of other 'homes' where they are fed, and in extreme situations more than one household may actually believe the cat belongs to them!

Solutions

When you move house, it is essential to keep your cat safely confined to the new home for at least a week before giving it access to the outside world. Ideally, take it out on a long lead and harness while it establishes a map of the immediate garden area, and keep the door open for its return. Increasingly confident behaviour will indicate when the cat is ready to go 'solo'.

Avoid high stress levels that might make a cat leave home; some cats cannot cope with multi-cat households, or continual disturbance from building work and the like.

Neutering male cats will generally reduce both their range size and potential for wandering.

A cat wearing a name tag and collar, or which has an identification chip, is less likely to be mistaken for a stray in need of a home by well-meaning near-neighbours or welfare organizations.

If you find well-meaning neighbours are also feeding your cat in the mistaken idea that it is homeless, a tactful conversation will often remedy the situation.

CAT TROUBLES

related areas...   17   48   49   64   70

Index

About the author

Recognized as one of the world's leading authorities on cats, naturalist and biologist Roger Tabor wrote and presented the BBC TV series *Cats* and *Understanding Cats*, which were shown on the Learning Channel and PBS in the USA, and on other networks around the world. He has appeared on numerous television programmes, and is a best-selling, award-winning author. Roger is also highly regarded for his pioneering studies of urban feral cats, and has actively worked on cat behaviour and ecology for over 30 years. He has travelled extensively, observing cats in over 25 countries around the world. A keen photographer, he takes the majority of the pictures in his books.

Acknowledgments

I have been helped over the years by innumerable kind people, whose assistance has been incorporated in the production of this book. I cannot possibly hope to thank everyone who has been involved, and I trust those that I do not mention by name will nonetheless know they have my thanks.

My grateful thanks to Dick Meadows and colleagues at the BBC, John Bowe, Colin Tennant and colleagues at Bowe-Tennant Productions, University of East London, White Notley Cats Protection and Cats Protection, Doris Westwood and the Fitzroy Sqare Frontagers & Garden's Committee, Mary Wyatt, Mike Jackson, Becky Robinson & Alley Cat Allies, UFAW, GCCF, TICA, Cairo Museum, British Museum, Debbie Rijnders & Stichting de Zwerfkat, Venice DINGO, Joan Hodge, Stuart Baldwin, and particular thanks to veterinary surgeon Alan Hatch.

Thanks also to Charlotte, Bob & Vally Hudson, Phillipa Spalding, Michael Harding, Mike Sutton, Robin & Georgie Kiashek, Rachel & Ralph Cooke, Sue Sanderman, Solvig Pfluger, Norman, Janet, John, Vikki & Milli Collins, Ken Tabor, Callie & Lauren Doherty, Ed & Malee Rose, Jean Murchison, Dawn Guliver, Steve & Margaret Cuthbert, Jean Renny, Rosie Alger & Barrie Street, Mira Bar-Hillel & Geoffrey Addison, Diane Slater, Jackie & Barry Wood, Anne Bailey, Bernice Mead, Barbara Castle, and to all cats and cat owners who have assisted my research, particularly my own cats Jeremy, Tabitha and Leroy. Thanks are due to Angela Weatherley, and to Jane Trollope and the David & Charles team. Special thanks to Liz Artindale for her considerable help and support, and for the fine addition of her photographs that stand alongside mine.

ROGER TABOR, 2005

Additional information on cats and Roger Tabor can be found at **www.worldofcats.net**

Picture credits

All photographs by Roger Tabor, except the following:

Liz Artindale: pp.6–7, 8–9, 13 bottom right, 14, 15, 16 top, 17, 18 right, 20 left, 21 top, 23 right, 24, 44 centre right, 48, 58, 63, 68, 76 left, 82 right, 85, 86, 87 right, 92 left, 96, 97 except top far right, 98 bottom far right, 99 except bottom far right, 102 left, 103, 105 left, 106 right, 107, 108 left, 110, 117, 123, 126 left, 131 left, 133 left, 135, 137 left.

John Bowe/Bowe-Tennant Productions with Roger Tabor: pp.37, 38–39, 51 except bottom right, 70 right top and bottom.

Michael Harding: p.95 top.

Mike Sutton: p.132 right.

Front cover and p.3 © Brand X Pictures/Alamy.

All artworks by Eva Melhuish.